This book is
dedicated to
**SATTY
ASHTON-JONES**
(Nee Singh)
1944-2014
who selflessly
supported both
patients and staff
at St John's for
50 of its 150 years.

SKIN

A HISTORY

150 YEARS OF
ST JOHN'S INSTITUTE OF DERMATOLOGY

THE AUTHOR

Jeremy Laurance is a writer on health issues. He is a former Health Editor of The Independent and was previously health correspondent of the The Times, Sunday Times, and Sunday Correspondent. He has covered the specialism for more than 20 years. He was named Specialist Writer of the Year in the 2011 British Press Awards.

We wish to thank all colleagues who have contributed to this celebratory book especially Gary Mulcahy for his help providing images, Andrew Griffiths for his editorial review, Anita Knowles and Megan Elliott who have kept everyone to task and Andrew Younger and Ana Comsa at AYA-Creative for their design skills. Designed and produced by Andrew Younger of AYA-Creative and Printed by Blue Sky Design & Print. Published by Guy's and St Thomas' NHS Foundation Trust. © Guy's and St Thomas' NHS Foundation Trust. No part of this publication may be reproduced by any means without prior written permission of the authors. A full list of acknowledgements is detailed on pages 127 and 128. **ISBN 978-0-9934493-0-7 Skin - A History - 150 Years of St John's Institute of Dermatology.**

CONTENTS

FOREWORD

The skin is our largest and most visible organ. It protects the body behind an impermeable outer covering but is itself constantly on view. Patients with skin diseases thus have nowhere to hide. They are condemned to suffer twice – once from the condition and secondly from the public reaction to it.

John Milton, who founded St John's Institute for Dermatology in 1863, understood this. Recognising that his patients had special needs, within two years he had established an evening clinic to cater for the "artisan classes" who risked dismissal from their employment if "it were known they were afflicted with a skin disease."

A sensitivity to the needs of its patients has distinguished St John's ever since. It was not the first hospital for skin diseases in the UK but it quickly established itself as the best. The flow of patients that started as a trickle slowly built up till tens of thousands were flocking through its doors.

Today, 150 years later, St John's is an internationally renowned clinical, research and educational Institute epitomising the tripartite mission of King's Health Partners, our Academic Health Science Centre, and providing a world class service to 10,000 new patients annually from around the country and the globe with the most complex, challenging skin conditions known to medicine.

It has pioneered new treatments and techniques, identified new conditions and deepened understanding of the mechanisms of disease. In doing so it has brought relief to hundreds of thousands of patients.

This book tells the sometimes turbulent story of St John's from its humble beginnings in two rooms in Soho, through its decades of struggle against medical hostility and financial disaster, to the development of the modern Institute with six specialist departments, providing cutting edge treatments and world-renowned research within London's flagship NHS foundation trust, Guy's and St Thomas'.

St John's is today at the forefront of modern, multidisciplinary medical care, poised to exploit breakthroughs in clinical genetics, immunology and personalised medicine that we confidently believe will pave the way to even greater successes over the next 150 years.

Sean Whittaker, Professor of Cutaneous Oncology, St John's Institute of Dermatology, September 2015

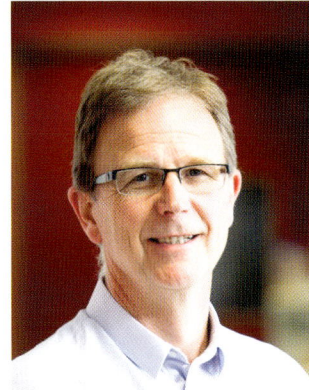

THE FIRST 150 YEARS

1 The Hospital at 49 Leicester Square (1887 - 1905) and 2 (1906 - 1935) 3 The Hospital at 5 Lisle Street (1935 - 1990)
4 The Hospital at St Thomas' Hospital (1990 - 2015) 5 The Hospital at Guy's (2015)

It was, by any standards, a difficult birth. St John's Hospital for Diseases of the Skin opened its doors to patients in 1863 – and almost closed them a year later after a dispute broke out among the staff. A second row nearly scuppered the construction of a new building a decade later and minor scandals beset the hospital for the remainder of the 19th century.

But by the beginning of the 20th century the hospital was treating 8,000 new patients a year, – "far ahead of its rivals in the number of patients it relieved," according to one account – had rebuilt its out-patients department at a cost of £10,000 and was rapidly becoming established as a national centre of excellence for skin diseases.

By the outbreak of World War II more than 65,000 patients a year were attending and the hospital had to annexe space in institutions up to eight miles away to cope with the demand.

Today it is one of the best known centres for the treatment and study of skin diseases in the world. It is staffed by 36 consultants (of whom six are professors) and 25 clinical nurse specialists who are leaders in their fields, treats 10,000 new patients with the most challenging skin conditions annually and has enjoyed more citations in the research literature than any comparable institution.

John Laws Milton

Its founder, **John Laws Milton**, was a surgeon whose career was cut short by hand eczema. The condition was severe enough to prevent him from operating and that experience appears to have triggered his interest in dermatology. He wanted London to have

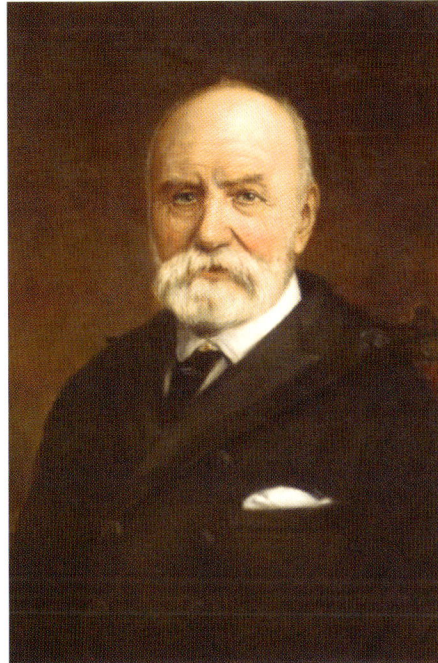

John Laws Milton, founder of St John's

a proper hospital for skin diseases and the project became his passion.

Born in 1820, he was in his 40s when he opened his "hospital" in two small rooms at 12 Church Street, Westminster (now Romilly Street, Soho). The hospital was named after St John the Divine and Milton was the only member of staff, attending patients once a week. Why he chose the name St John is unknown.

The hospital was supported by voluntary contributions and its patron was **Lord Chesterfield**. A gold medal awarded annually to outstanding

postgraduate diplomates of St John's still bears Chesterfield's name.

It was not the first hospital for skin diseases in London – there were at least two, the Hospital for Diseases of the Skin in Blackfriars and the Western Dispensary for Diseases of the Skin in Fitzroy Square – but it outlasted them both. The former founded in 1841 closed in 1948 at the start of the NHS and the latter founded in 1852 closed in 1946.

Within two years St John's had moved to 45 Leicester Square – then a neglected, weed-infested garden – where it remained for two decades. Clinics were held daily in the afternoons, with an evening clinic laid on once a week to enable the "artisan classes" to attend "without it being known that they are afflicted with a skin disease." That way they might avoid dismissal from their employment.

It was an indication of the importance of the emerging specialism of dermatology in providing relief to patients who suffered twice over with their disease – once from the condition itself and twice from the revulsion it typically inspired in others.

The flow of patients started as a trickle but later built up until tens of thousands were flocking through its doors. In its first ten years, St John's treated 20,000 patients. As its reputation grew so did its imitators and London was suddenly afflicted with a rash of skin hospitals. But by 1897 it was said to be "far ahead of the others in the number of patients relieved."

Early battles

Its success did not come easily. John Milton was not a member of the establishment and did not have a

Tilbury Fox

Erasmus Wilson

high reputation among his peers. Indeed he stirred up controversy and, as already mentioned, the hospital was stalked by scandal during its early decades. There was resentment from generalists about the growth of specialist hospitals in London which were felt to be unnecessarily duplicating the work of specialist clinics in general hospitals for financial gain.

Critics demanded to know why there was a need for a stand-alone skin hospital when there was a perfectly serviceable skin clinic at the local hospital down the road.

In 1864, a year after opening St John's, Milton was joined on the staff by three colleagues – two physicians and a second surgeon by the names of **Tilbury Fox**, MD, **J. Mill Frodsham**, MD, and **Erasmus Wilson**, FRS. These were significant medical figures and on 29 October that year, The Lancet described the "formation of a new establishment for skin diseases called (though for what special cutaneous reason we know not) St John's Hospital."

If Milton thought he and his hospital were on the road to fame and fortune, he was sadly mistaken. He had published a book about the controversial subject of spermatorrhoea – the involuntary and unwanted discharge of semen – and was accused of abusing his position by holding a lucrative clinic at St John's for the treatment of the condition.

What aroused the ire of the medical establishment was that he described himself on the title page of the 7th edition of his pamphlet, On Spermatorrhoea, as "Surgeon to St John's Hospital". This was too much for his trio of new colleagues who did not want to be associated with the "disease" nor with Milton's pamphlet. A critical and hostile report appeared in the Lancet followed by a second a week later. His colleagues resigned *en masse*.

By 1867, the breach was repaired and two of the three resigning members were back on the staff. Milton was a prolific author, contributing regularly to the Journal of Cutaneous Medicine and Diseases of the Skin edited by Erasmus Wilson.

Among his writings were: On bubo; Death in the Pipe; The stream of life on our Globe; Spermatorrhoea, its results and complications; The pathology and treatment of diseases of the skin; Tartar Emetic in Inflammation of Cellular Tissues.

He became a fellow of the Medical Society of London, a member of the Harveian Society and a corresponding member of the New York Dermatological Society.

49 Leicester Square

The hospital moved twice in the early years, first to No 45 Leicester Square in 1865 and then to No 49, described as a "light and airy" building. By then the square had been renovated and the weeds removed providing the in-patients with a "pleasant place to exercise and stroll."

In 1873, plans were underway to build a new hospital but were scuppered by another hostile article in The Lancet renewing its attack on the specialist hospitals (exemplifying both "error and egotism") and criticising the proposed collection of £75,000 for the building. This would "dissipate public money on the creation of special buildings" which would be better spent on the creation of "special departments in the large [general] hospitals".

Further vitriolic letters appeared, detrimental to the hospital's reputation, and an inquiry was launched into the workings of its haphazard financial accounts. This led, in 1874, to a decision to draw up a Code of Rules and Regulations for St Johns.

By the mid-1870s, the hospital had an imposing list of Royal Governors. But a crisis was never far away and the next one erupted over the hospital's habit of giving priority to patients who paid. The British Medical Journal attacked the practice and a dispute broke out between the Hospital Board and the medical staff, resulting in resignations and

Leicester Square in 1874 after the opening of the new garden providing patients with a "pleasant place to stroll."

Cartoon published in Judy in 1899 shows Mr Milton trying to encourage the Princess of Wales to remain a Patroness of the hospital.

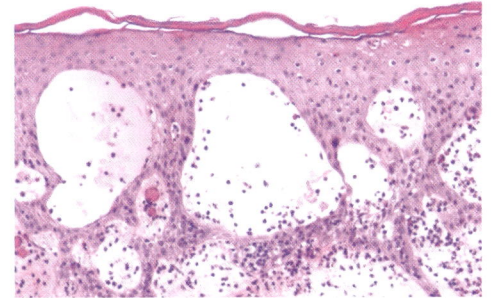

Herpes Gestationis, a skin disease in pregnancy, described by Milton in 1872

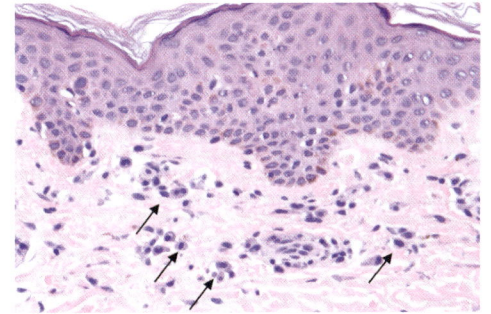

Giant urticaria, described by Milton in 1872

actions for libel. With the hospital struggling to make ends meet and avoid financial ruin, the sustained attacks in the press did nothing to help.

Scandal continued to dog the hospital through the following decade. An appeal to upgrade the building in Leicester Square raised £523 but the Board was later obliged to report that "the proposed alterations were not carried out, although the amount subscribed for the purpose was wholly absorbed." Donations dropped off and the Princess of Wales, later to become Queen Alexandra, resigned as royal patron. In 1899 a cartoon

appeared in Judy showing Milton attempting to cajole the Princess into remaining as a patron of the hospital.

Through all his 35 years at the hospital Milton seems to have played a controlling role in the background, shepherding it through its troubles and scandals. He also found time to practise medicine, describing two diseases – *Herpes Gestationes* in 1872 and *Giant Urticaria* in 1876.

His recommended treatment for a case of *Herpes Gestationes* involved: "A quart bottle of stout daily, with at least one or two glasses of wine, rum, and

milk at night and beef tea ad libitum".

In another case, he wrote: "She could not bear even zinc ointment, and I therefore directed that she should be covered from head to foot with linen rags dipped in fresh melted suet."

In a eulogy published in The Echo on 25 April, 1873, the hospital's tenth anniversary, Charles Mercier, vice chairman, wrote: "It was started by Mr J L Milton, a surgeon who had given diseases of the skin his special attention, and who was struck with the misery those diseases entailed. With the co-operation of several friends he took and

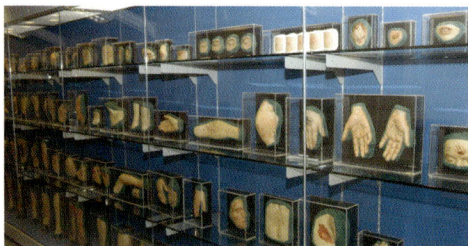

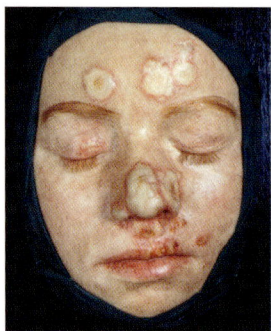

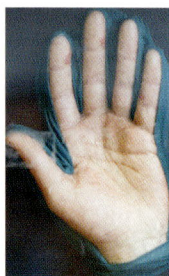

The wax moulages of skin diseases are the work of Alice Gretener (1905-1986) who attended St Johns in 1936 as a medical artist. These compliment the wax moulages in the Guys Museum by Joseph Towne

furnished a small place in Westminster. The subscription list did not cover more than a quarter's rent, yet, from that time to the present, the St John's Hospital has continued and has gained the confidence of the thinking portion of the public to an unexampled extent .... For ten years Mr Milton has continued to give his services as a professional man to the hospital and devoted all his spare time and much from his private practice to promoting its influence. That London shall have a proper Skin Diseases Hospital is the one idea of his life."

The School of Dermatology

On 8 October, 1864, an advertisement for an inaugural lecture at St John's appeared in the Medical Times and Gazette. It announced that clinical lectures would be delivered throughout the session and quoted a price of three guineas for "three months attendance of hospital practice".

A report in the British Medical Journal on 22 October congratulated the organisers on the "numbers who attended" and the "ambitious and energetic" way they were pursuing their aims. But two weeks later, Mr Milton's colleagues had resigned leaving him as sole member of staff. It is hence doubtful that the course of lectures was ever completed.

In 1876-77 a new course of lectures was announced – this time free to doctors and medical students. The Annual Report of that year hints at the scale of the hospital's ambition. "The Committee trust that this will be a step towards providing in London a National School of Dermatology."

In 1885 the School of Dermatology at St John's was inaugurated. In-patient accommodation was moved to Markham Square, Chelsea and the space vacated at Leicester Square converted into a Microscope Room and library.

Three years later, in 1888, women medical students were admitted for the first time. A fee was quoted of two guineas a term – the earlier commitment to free courses had proved a step too far. More courses were added over the ensuing decades.

Robert Koch

A centre of learning

The first research was carried out in 1890 when the treatment for tuberculosis discovered by **Robert Koch**, who won the Nobel prize in 1905, was trialled in cases of *Lupus vulgaris*, the most common skin infection associated with the then widespread disease. Lupus vulgaris was a virulent, ulcerating condition that produced a profusion of nodules, most often on the face and neck. Professor Koch's "fluid", described as "brown and viscid, the colour of iodine" was delivered direct to the hospital by him for the treatment of what was regarded as the "most disfiguring of all" skin diseases. A committee of three, including Milton, was established to "enquire into Professor Koch's discovery and report thereon."

The Annual Report for 1890 noted: "The investigation with its anxious supervision and hourly observations, has entailed much labour on the whole executive and involved a considerable outlay." Its outcome is unfortunately not recorded.

Meanwhile the courses run at the hospital were proving successful. In 1893, the **Earl of Chesterfield** established a prize of a gold medal presented to the person attending the lectures who showed the most promise. The following year **Morgan Dockrell** was appointed Chesterfield lecturer. In 1901 there were 194 entries for the 26 lectures offered, with an average attendance of 40 at each. Dockrell declared the London School of Dermatology established on March 1 of that year but it was not formally inaugurated until more than 20 years later.

Other institutions were becoming restive at St John's success. The President of the Royal College of Physicians challenged Dockrell to explain why specimen sections taken from patients were not sent to the "recognised institutions" so the clinical diagnosis could be confirmed.

Dockrell replied that "the pathologist attached to the ordinary hospital was incapable of diagnosing different skin diseases as they presented themselves under the microscope."

He added that dermatologists from the large hospitals were coming to St John's to learn how to answer the questions from their students who had trained there. It was a rap on the knuckles for the medical establishment.

Dockrell died in 1920 having been on the staff of St John's for 32 years and Chesterfield lecturer for 25. Three years later, in 1923, the London School of Dermatology was formed. But it was still controversial and some invited to join, declined. **Wilfred Fox**, one of the eventual founders,

Sir Malcolm Morris   James Herbert Stowers   Sir Ernest Graham Little   John Macleod

described how **Sir Malcolm Morris**, another of its backers, approached him to support the venture.

"He cornered me one day and asked if I would go on the staff of St John's. At that time the hospital had not a very good name and I hesitated but he reassured me and said they wanted me on the staff to make it respectable."

Others too declined the invitation to join, including **Hugh Barber** and **Archibald Gray**. But thanks to the perseverance of a few stalwart supporters led by **James Stowers** who instigated the school, it flourished. From 1923 the reputation

of both hospital and school steadily improved. Tribute was paid to Stowers' role in boosting the standing of St John's in his obituary in 1931. **Graham Little** described his personal debt to the man who had brought the hospital and school firmly into the mainstream.

"Thirty years ago when I was beginning my dermatological life, St John's was under a cloud and I was personally and strenuously warned by my seniors that to accept an appointment at St John's was to court ostracism. To overcome the deeply ingrained prejudices and unite...members of all the teaching hospitals in London was an effort which few persons could have undertaken with success. It is a lasting monument to the affection which Stowers, with his modest kindliness, inspired that he was able, by his personal influence, to reconcile discordances and to bring so many conflicting views into harmony and united action."

It still had far to go. In 1925, **John MacLeod** was appointed to the staff, who successfully organised the Department of Pathology, set up laboratories and put skin pathology firmly on the medical map. It has been said that without him St John's would have remained little more than a dispensary.

Patient treated with Koch's fluid for Lupus Vulgaris

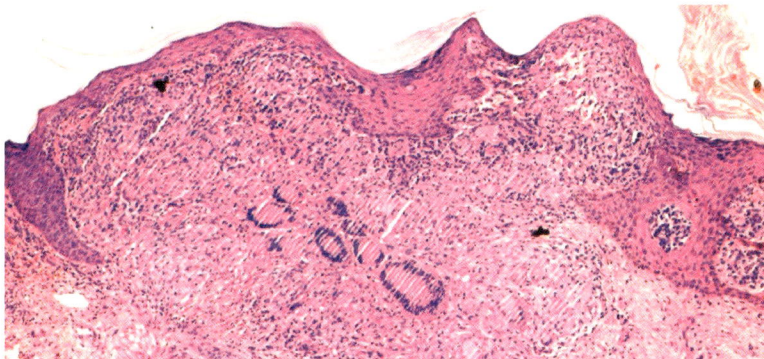

Lupus Vulgaris – the commonest skin infection associated with tuberculosis

Honours Board at Lisle Street

The honours board lists (best reading):

PRESIDENTS

1912-14	MORGAN DOCKRELL
1914-15	WILLIAM GRIFFITH
1915-16	JOHN L BUNCH
1916-17	W. KNOWSLEY SIBLEY
1917-19	WILLIAM GRIFFITH
1918-19	A. T. BREMNER
1920-23	R PROSSER WHITE
1923-24	JOHN L BUNCH
1924-25	W. KNOWSLEY SIBLEY

St John's Hospital Dermatological Society

1925-28	WILFRID FOX
1928-30	ERNEST DORE
1930-32	A. C. ROXBURGH
1932-34	J. M. H. MAC LEOD
1934-36	J. E. M. WIGLEY
1936-38	W. N. GOLDSMITH
1938-42	R. T. BRAIN
1948-50	H CORSI
1950-52	G B DOWLING
1952-54	L. FORMAN
1954-56	A. D. PORTER
1956-58	GORDON MITCHELL-HEGGS

1959-60	Dr BRIAN RUSSELL
1960-62	Dr HENRY HABER
1962-63	Dr F RAY BETTLEY
1963-64	Dr H J WALLACE
1964-65	Dr H.T.H. WILSON
1965-66	Dr S. C. GOLD
1966-67	Dr D S WILKINSON
1967-68	Dr G C WELLS
1968-69	Dr H. T. CALVERT
1969-70	Dr R. H. MEARA
1970-71	Dr M. FEIWEL
1971-72	Professor C.D. CALNAN
1972-73	Dr R.J. CAIRNS
1973-74	Dr F.D. SAMMAN
1974-75	Dr K.V. SANDERSON
1975-76	Professor E. WILSON JONES
1976-77	Dr I. SARKANY
1977-78	Professor M.W. GREAVES
1978-79	Dr HARVEY BAKER
1979-80	Dr ETAIN CRONIN
1980-81	Dr C.M. RIDLEY
1981-82	Dr R.S. WELLS
1982-83	Dr M.A. SMITH
1983-84	Dr M.M. BLACK
1984-85	Dr D.D. MUNRO
1985-86	Dr G.M. LEVENE
1986-97	Dr JULIA P. ELLIS

1987-88	Dr.W.A.D. GRIFFITHS
1988-89	Dr. TREVOR ROBINSON
1989-90	Dr R.A.J. EADY
1990-91	Dr. ANTHONY du VIVIER
1991-92	Dr. R.J.G RYCROFT
1992-93	Dr. RICHARD STAUGHTON
1993-94	Prof. R.J. HAY
1994-95	Dr PETER HUDSON

1995-96	Dr. NEIL P. SMITH
1996-97	Dr CHARLES R. DARLEY
1997-98	Dr. J.L.M. HAWK
1998-99	Dr. MARTIN P. JAMES
1999-00	Dr. DAVID McGIBBON
2000-01	Dr. VALERIE NEILD
2001-02	Dr. IAN R. WHITE
2002-03	Dr. ELISABETH HIGGINS

5 Lisle Street

After 70 years on Leicester square, in 1935 the hospital moved a few yards north to No 5 Lisle Street, a grand renaissance style building with a distinctive stepped gable which is now a listed building.

Little more than a decade later, St John's admittance into the medical mainstream was finally confirmed on the inauguration of the National Health Service in 1948, when it was designated as one of 14 Postgraduate Teaching Hospitals.

It quickly outgrew its new premises, expanding into the building behind at 26-28 Gerrard Street in 1950, and taking over the neighbouring building No 30, a former nightclub, in 1962. It also rented premises opposite.

Its library, run by **Hildegard Freyhan**, was renowned. She compiled a list of all the books, and scanned the medical literature, providing a digest once a month in *The Bulletin*. It proved an invaluable aid for busy clinicians who needed to keep up with the latest developments in the specialty.

St John's also acquired renown amongst a different clientele – the prostitutes who frequented Lisle Street and were often driven off the streets by police. It is reputed that the Lisle Street porters who held the post from the 1950s gave them sanctuary and unofficially provided treatments.

While there was much activity at Lisle Street, the in-patient wards were not so centrally located. Beds had been provided in Chelsea, in Finchley and in a converted private house at 238 (later 262) Uxbridge Road. Between 28 and 50 patients were accommodated there from 1895 until it was damaged by bombing in September 1940.

There were no in-patient beds for the remainder of the war. In 1952, 16 were provided in Hackney, in a disused section of the Eastern Fever Hospital, Homerton. Their numbers progressively increased in subsequent years to 69 in 1960. New research laboratories were set up and the department of photobiology established under Professor **Ian Magnus**. But the location, eight miles from Leicester Square, was far from ideal.

St John's in the NHS

In 1946 the Institute of Dermatology led by Sir Archibald Gray took over the London School of Dermatology which 26 years earlier the then plain Dr Gray had declined to join

In 1951, three years after the foundation of the NHS, **Geoffrey Dowling** replaced Sir Archibald as part time director of the Institute and, with the help of the Dean, **J E M Wigley**, steered St John's through its formative years as an NHS teaching institution.

Dowling was 60 but that did not dampen his enthusiasm, and he became a key influence on young dermatologists whose confidence he boosted. An obituary in the South African Medical Journal (he was born in Cape Town and died in 1976) declared: "His greatest work was culling and welding together a large circle of dermatologists linked by respect, loyalty and devotion to their chosen field."

He was a charismatic and popular figure. The obituary noted: "He passed on more ideas than he worked on himself and let others take the credit." His name is commemorated in the Dowling Club and Dowling Day Centre. His main research interest was *sclerodoma* and related conditions and he jointly discovered the curative value of high dose Vitamin D in *lupus vulgaris*.

Academically, however, he was eclipsed by his student, **Charles Calnan**, who in 1961 was appointed the first Professor of Dermatology in London. The University of London established its first chair in

Etain Cronin, consultant in the Contact Clinic (left) with Hywel Williams (later Professor – in white shirt, front row), Lisle Street in the late 1980s

dermatology at St John's in recognition of its status as a component Institute of the Postgraduate Medical Federation.

Calnan never became a full time academic, and continued his clinical work. His specialist interest was *contact dermatitis* and he established the Department of Industrial Dermatoses (originally called the "Contact Clinic").

He began keeping photographic records of all skin conditions, built up a world class skin allergy testing unit and established St John's as an internationally recognised centre of clinical and research excellence.

Among his appointments was that of **John Turk**, who pinpointed the role of lymphocytes in the regional lymph nodes in the development of *cutaneous contact sensitisation*, and **Ian Magnus**, who with colleagues defined the inborn error of metabolism in *erythropoietic protoporphyria* and pioneered the development of the monochromator (see Chapter 3).

Links were established with US institutions and members of the institute travelled across the Atlantic for training in new technologies while foreign specialists came to St John's.

Calnan also built up the teaching at St John's, including the establishment of informal Saturday morning clinics where "hot" cases – patients whose symptoms had erupted and might disappear in a few days – were discussed. These were usually hosted by a senior registrar and the clinics proved to be a popular and effective teaching method.

Calnan retired in 1975. His successor, Professor **Malcom Greaves**, extended and developed the research facilities at St John's, winning major programme grants from the Medical Research

Geoffrey Dowling

Charles Calnan

Ian Magnus

Malcolm Greaves

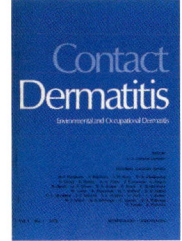

First edition (1975) edited by Charles Calnan

Council and the Wellcome Trust to build new laboratories at Homerton. They included a mass spectrometry unit for research into the molecular mechanisms of inflammation, Greaves' special interest, which later yielded a breakthrough in understanding *chronic urticaria* (see Chapter 6).

Guy's and St Thomas'

In the years after the war, St John's consisted of two administratively distinct but closely associated components. They were the St John's Hospital for Diseases of the Skin, with its own board of governors

answerable directly to the Minister of Health, and the Institute of Dermatology, financed via the British

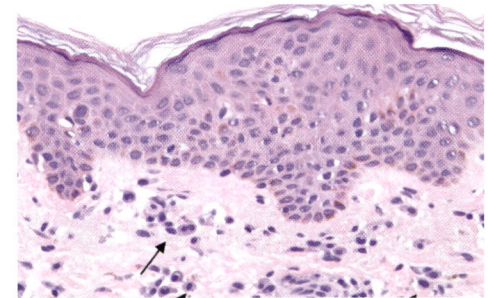

Urticaria

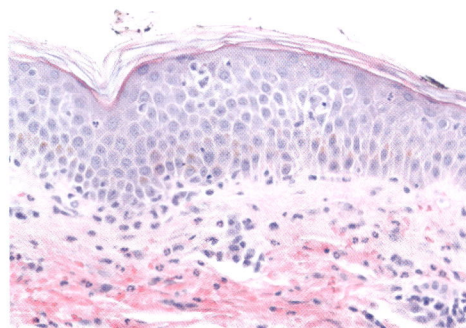

Irritant contact dermatitis

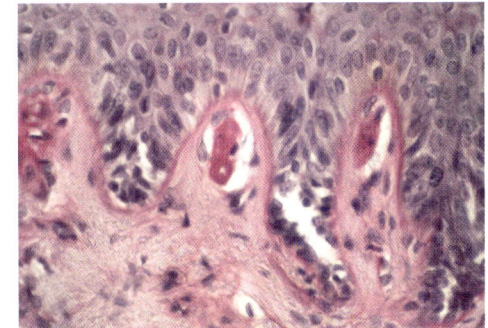

Protoporphyria

Cartoon by Neil Smith, consultant skin pathologist, showing members of St John's staff, 1992

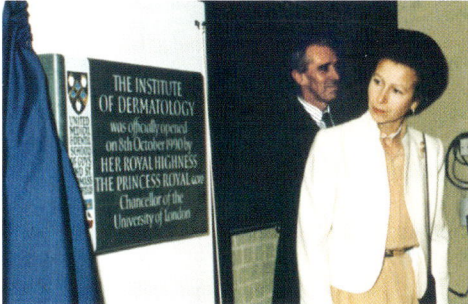
HRH The Princess Royal opening the Institute of Dermatology

regular meetings for consultants to discuss clinical challenges and new developments with doctors in training. It also runs a wide range of popular courses for GPs and other health professionals.

The focus of education is increasingly international. The MSc course in clinical dermatology attracts many doctors and healthcare workers from countries where there is little or no local expertise. The MSc programme in Diagnostic Dermatopathology is the first postgraduate programme of its kind in the UK and in Europe. St John's runs the UK's largest skin pathology centre.

Many of its senior staff have joint appointments at both the university and the trust. This is seen as one of its particular strengths – straddling the academic and clinical communities – providing a unique environment in which researchers and clinicians can collaborate to pursue patient-based research.

Jonathan Barker, professor of Clinical Dermatology at St John's put it succinctly: "It is very unusual – and it works."

Postgraduate Medical Federation by the University of London.

Following Lord Flowers report in the early 1980s which advised the Government to amalgamate smaller postgraduate institutes and their associated hospitals, St John's gradually relocated to St Thomas' Hospital in the late 1980s. In-patient wards and some laboratories at Homerton moved first in 1987, followed by the out-patient facilities at Lisle Street, which closed. By 1990, St John's Institute of Dermatology – renamed to include both the hospital and the institute – was back on a single site for the first time in more than 50 years.

In 1993, St Thomas' merged with Guy's Hospital to form a single NHS trust. By 2005, some departments of St John's had moved from St Thomas' to Guy's, and the rest are due to follow by 2015.

Education and Research

Today, St John's has close research links with King's College London. It runs monthly training courses for post-graduates and the St John's Society holds

St John's runs training courses for post-graduates from the UK and overseas

The Future

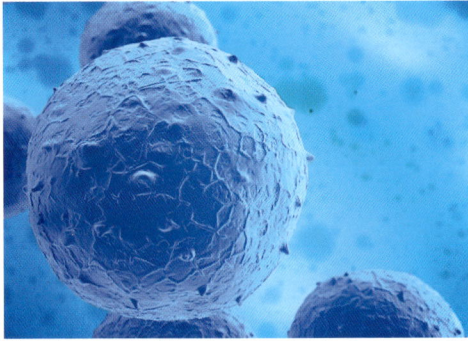

Today, dermatology operates in a more complex medical landscape

Through its merger with Guy's and St Thomas' NHS Foundation Trust, St John's has entered a new era – the era of multidisciplinary medicine. For 150 years it has served as a focal point for the development of treatments for patients with very challenging skin conditions drawn from around the world. By attracting a critical mass of specialists with expertise in the field, it provided a unique environment in which doctors with ideas and expertise could flourish and innovate to improve the clinical specialty of dermatology and the care of patients.

Today, as part of a large NHS Trust, St John's has had to redefine itself. It continues to be a focal point for the development of dermatology but in a more complex, sophisticated medical landscape. No specialty can grow in isolation. The merger with Guy's and St Thomas' provided the opportunity for integration with other closely related specialties including rheumatology *(Lupus, connective tissue disease)*, other cancer specialties, allergy services and clinical genetics.

Professor **Sean Whittaker** said: "Patients do not any longer have diseases defined by the organ affected. They have complex conditions with multiple causes that require expertise from multiple specialties. Patients with chronic inflammatory skin disease will now be managed in close conjunction with patients with chronic inflammatory diseases of the joints and connective tissue. They have the same mechanisms of disease and are treated with the same drugs. Patients with eczema will be managed alongside those with food allergies. The days when diseases were managed in silos, based on '-ologies', are over."

The modern treatment of skin cancer involves input from physicians, plastic surgeons and haematologists. Childhood skin disease requires input from general paediatricians, paediatric allergists and clinical geneticists. Developments in stratified personalised medicine will require inputs from genetics, immunology and therapeutics.

Professor Whittaker said: "Throughout its history, St John's has provided a focal point to bring other dermatologists together. Now, in addition, it is providing a focal point to bring other specialties together. Its integration into England's flagship NHS Foundation Trust, Guy's and St Thomas', has put it right at the forefront of modern, multidisciplinary medical care."

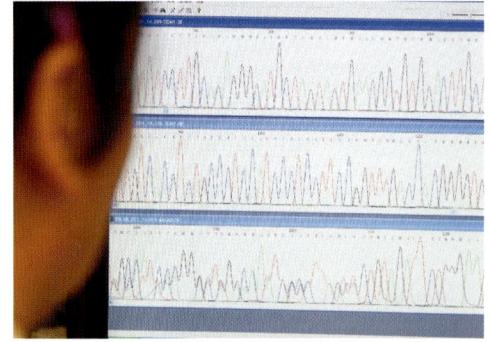

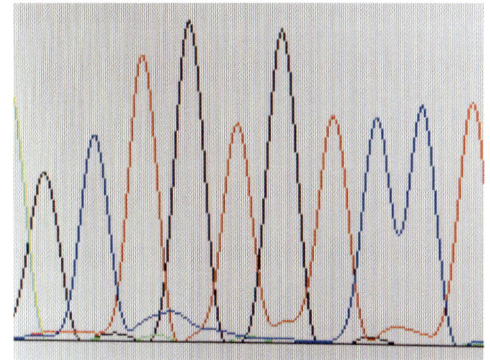

By attracting a critical mass of specialists, St John's provides a unique environment in which doctors can innovate to improve care

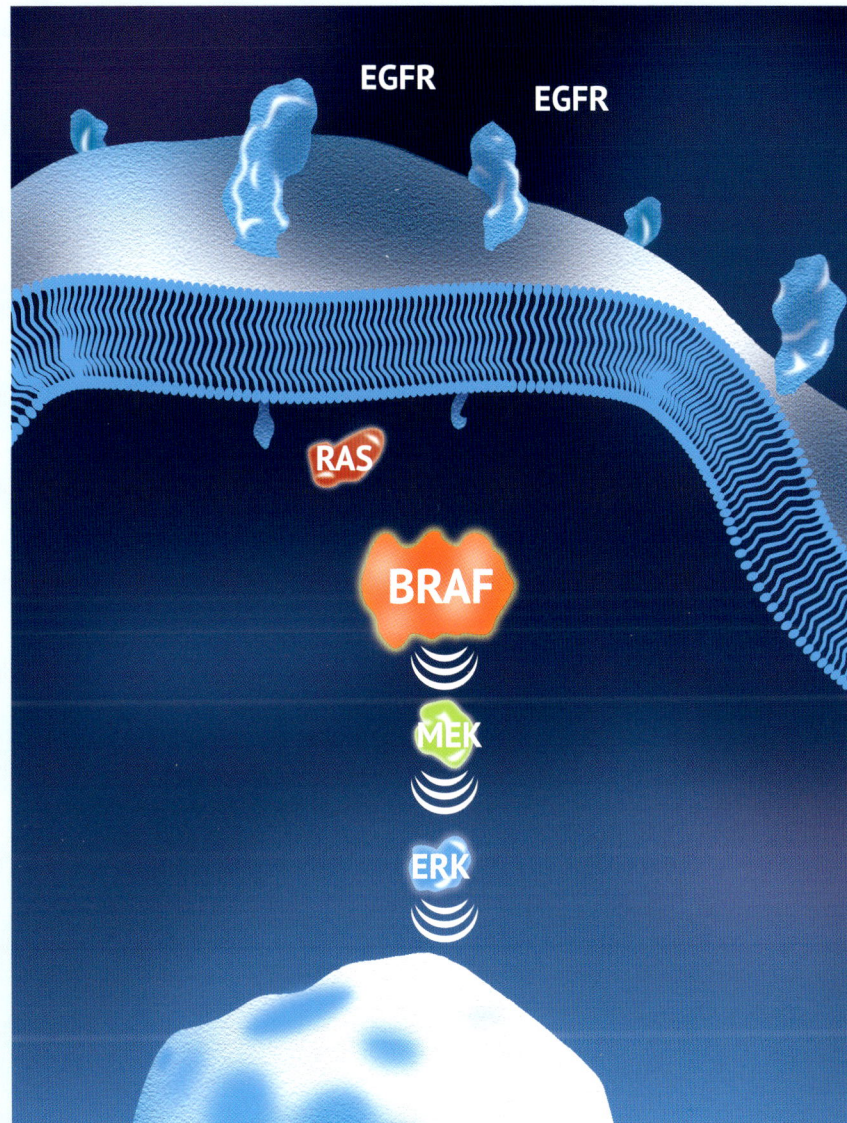

Genetic Analysis has shown that 60 per cent of melanomas have a BRAF mutation and 20 per cent a NRAS mutation. See Chapter 5 on Cutaneous Oncology

THE ROLE OF INHERITANCE AND THE CARE OF CHILDREN

Dry skin – the sort that itches, peels, flakes or cracks in cold weather – is extremely common. As many as one in ten of the population – five to ten million people – suffer from it at some stage. The cosmetics industry, with its emollient creams and lotions, is founded on it.

Some people have a more serious condition known as *ichthyosis* in which the skin is dry, thickened and scaly. Ichthyosis is derived from the Greek, meaning "fish scales", a reference to the characteristic appearance of the skin. The commonest type, accounting for 95 per cent of cases, is *ichthyosis vulgaris* which affects an estimated 800,000 people in Britain. It is mostly mild and in many cases mistaken for normal dry skin but rare types of ichthyosis can be severe and even life threatening.

Ichthyosis is a genetic skin disease, passed down the generations. There are an estimated 5,000 genetic diseases in all, of which around one third involve the skin. The best hope for patients suffering from these diseases is to identify the gene (or genes) that is the culprit and to develop a therapy based on that.

That is the task of the Paediatrics and Genetics department headed by Professor **John McGrath**. He is a gene hunter with a collection of scalps on his belt. To take one example, he and his team investigated *lipoid proteinosis,* a rare condition affecting one in 300,000 people which causes scarring and infiltration (thickening and hardening of the skin) and found the gene that caused it, *ECM1 (extracellular matrix protein 1).* Working on this protein, he then found a link to a much more common inflammatory skin condition, *lichen*

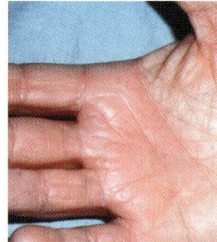
Ichthyosis

Ichthyosis Vulgaris

Lichen Sclerosus

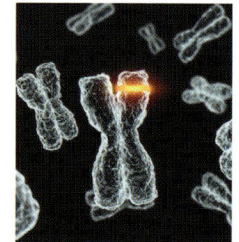
Chromosome Mutation

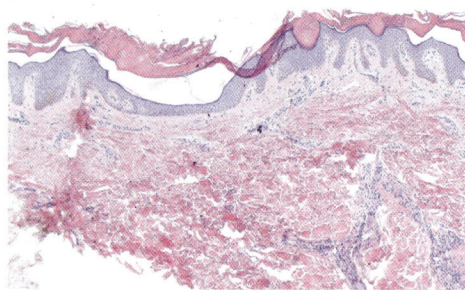

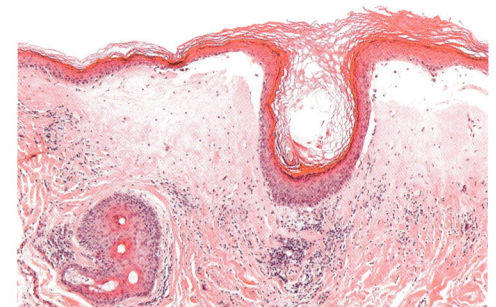

One in ten people – five to ten million – suffer from dry skin but some have a more serious conditions. Ichthyosis Vulgaris (left) affects around 800,000 people in Britain and Lichen Sclerosis (right) affects 200,000

sclerosus, which affects one in 300 people. The breakthrough in understanding led to new approaches to treating both diseases.

Professor McGrath and colleagues have since discovered several single gene mutations that are the cause of other skin diseases and opened the way for the development of new and more effective therapies.

At the same time the clinical service of paediatric dermatology offered at St John's has expanded rapidly since the mid-2000s. Prior to 2007, there was one paediatric clinic a month for the severest cases run by a consultant from Great Ormond Street Hospital for Sick Children.

The gene that causes lipoid proteinosis: ECM1

Today, the St John's clinic is designated as a national centre for the treatment of highly specialised paediatric skin disease. Last year, under consultant dermatologist **Jemima Mellerio**, it saw 2,000 patients.

"Until 2007, we used to get the children, babies with eczema and all the rest and put them in with the adults. Now that seems extraordinary," she said.

History

John McGrath

Geoffrey Dowling

Bob Meara

George Wells

Robin Eady at work in the 1960s

The origins of St John's expertise in genetics can be traced back to the 1950s when dermatologists from around London used to meet at the hospital, then in Lisle Street, to discuss unusual cases. "It was the collection of these cases and their careful description that laid the groundwork for future advance," said Professor McGrath.

Geoffrey Dowling, consultant and director of St Johns from 1951-56, described with registrar **Bob Meara** a form of the blistering skin disease *Epidermolysis Bullosa* (EB, see below) since called *Dowling-Meara EB simplex*.

R S Wells – known as Charlie – developed prototype classifications for the different types of

EB and ichthyosis. He was also an inspirational teacher, raised money to upgrade the dermatology section of Guy's medical museum to become a "teaching laboratory" and by the early 1980s St John's was producing one quarter of all the dermatologists in the country.

By then **Robin Eady**, another pioneer, was using

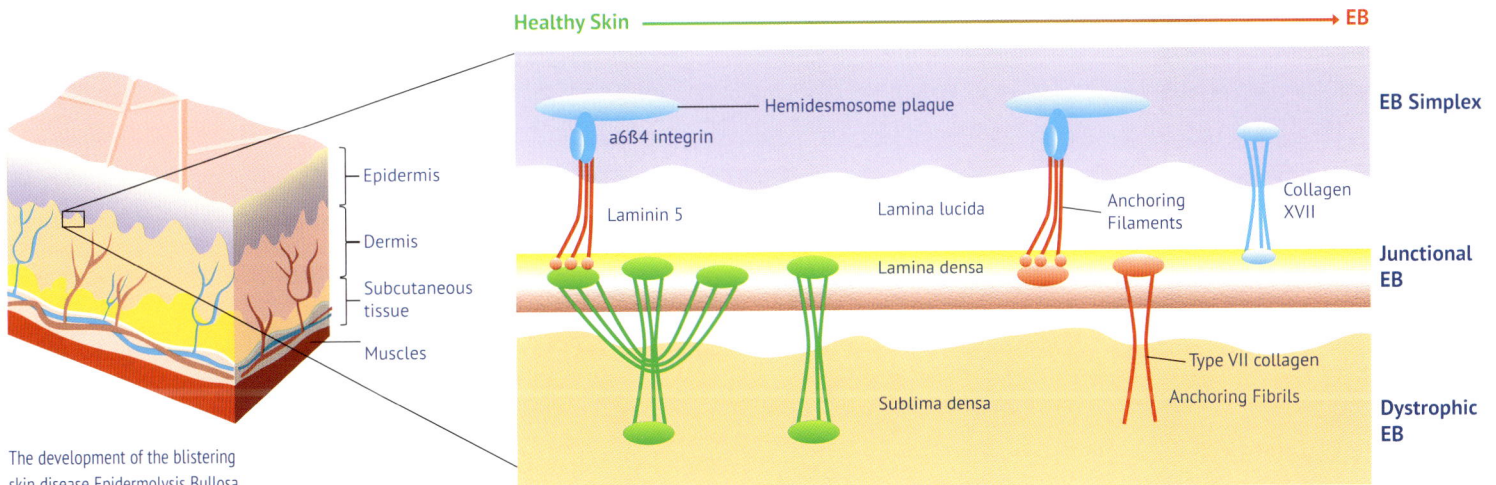

The development of the blistering skin disease Epidermolysis Bullosa

electron microscopy to see inside cells and inspect their structure. It was a long laborious process, but it led ultimately to quicker diagnosis through the introduction of *immunohistochemistry* (staining techniques), reducing the wait for results from three weeks to three days.

Eady, working with obstetricians, also pioneered the development of foetal skin biopsy – taking tiny skin samples from babies in the womb to examine for EB. The test was offered to parents who already had an affected child to give them the option of a termination. But the biopsy could not be done until 16 weeks, very late in the pregnancy. Foetal skin biopsy has now largely been superseded by *chorionic villus sampling*, taking a tiny sample from the placenta, which is carried out at 10-11 weeks and has already been applied to over 400 couples at St John's.

Nevertheless, this still left parents carrying an affected baby facing the heartrending decision of whether to seek a termination. It would have been far better to make the diagnosis before the mother became pregnant.

With the development of single cell *polymerase chain reaction (PCR)* technology, which could amplify a single piece of DNA by several orders of magnitude, pre-natal diagnosis became possible in the late 1990s. Parents could opt for in-vitro fertilisation (IVF) with pre-implantation diagnosis to select unaffected embryos for replacement in the womb. It was the natural extension of Eady's work

Eady, who was awarded an MBE in the New Year Honours 2014, was also a pioneer in a different way. He is the world's longest surviving kidney failure patient, at the time of writing, who as a medical student in 1963 flew to North America for treatment. He was so weak he had to be carried off the Boeing 707. He spent 24 years on dialysis and the last 26 with a kidney transplant.

Indirect immunohistochemistry and immunofluorescence methods

Pre-natal diagnosis of certain skin diseases became possible with the development of polymerase chain reaction (PCR) technology

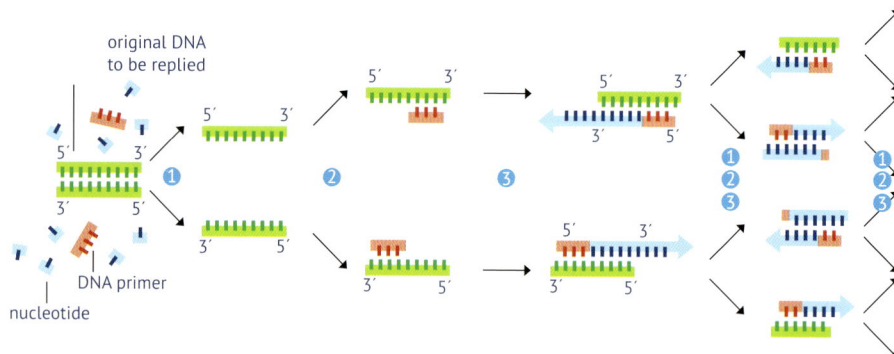

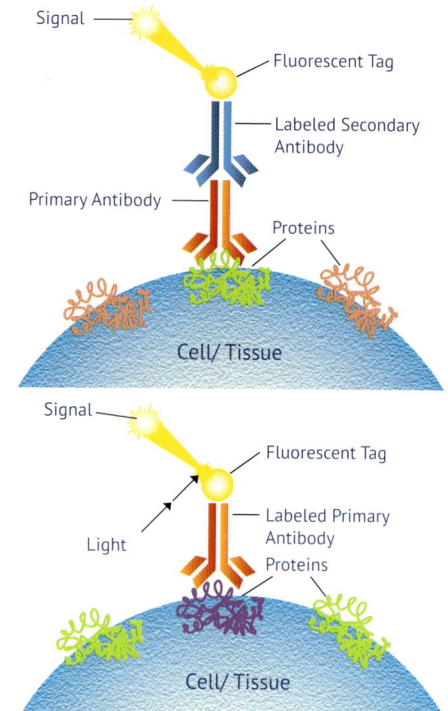

Genetic breakthrough

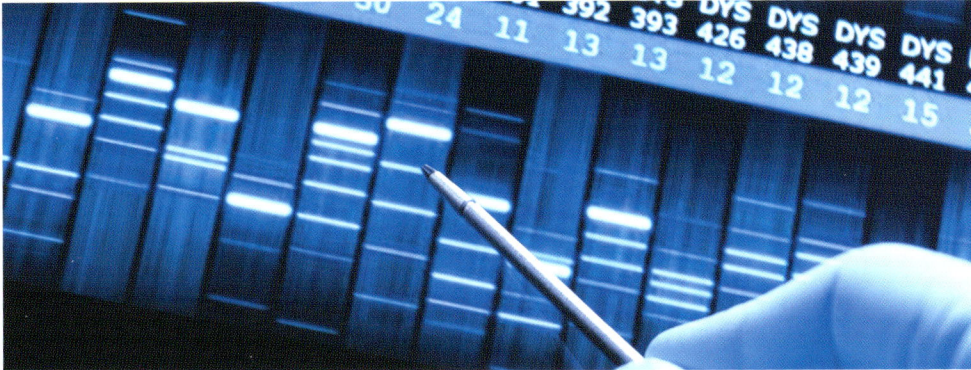

"It was going through the analyser and I could see there was an exciting mutation. It was a Eureka moment. We had discovered a new disease" – Professor John McGrath

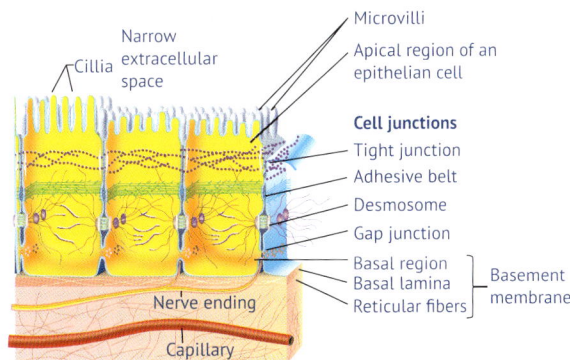

Plakophilin 1 Protein

In 1995, McGrath, who returned to St John's from a sojourn in the US, began his gene hunting in earnest. He established a molecular diagnostics laboratory and raised money for an automated gene sequencer, then regarded as a "new-fangled" piece of kit.

As it was being installed, McGrath pulled a tissue sample from his "special bottom draw" of mystery patients, to use as a test.

"It was going through the analyser and I could see the company technician frowning. He thought there was a malfunction. But I could see something exciting was unfolding - there was an exciting frame-shift mutation. It was a Eureka moment – we had found a new disease."

The sample in the sequencer was from a patient with *ectodermal dysplasia-skin fragility syndrome* and it had revealed the cause to be a demosomal gene disorder resulting from a mutation in plakophilin 1. It was the world's first genetic disorder of cell attachment complexes called *desmosomes*. After McGrath published his findings

in 1997 the condition subsequently became recognised as a form of *EB*.

Over the next 15 years, McGrath examined the structure, function and protein composition of

Special Characteristics of Epithelia-Cell Junction

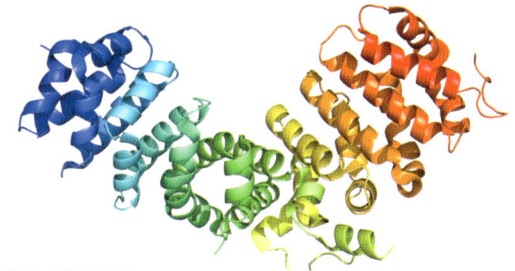

Desmosome

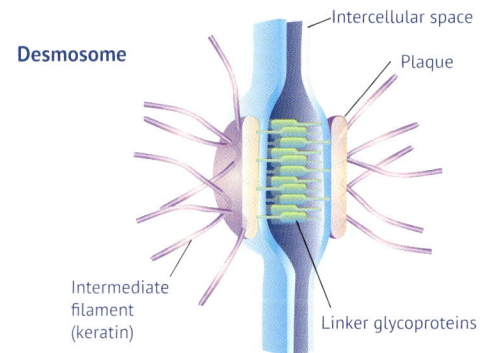

Desmosomes: Anchoring junctions bind adjacent cells together and help form an internal tension-reducing network of fibers.

tissue samples from a range of patients to gain some idea of what was going wrong in order to target the search for the genetic culprit with what is known as the "candidate gene" approach. With larger families where several members were affected, genetic linkage studies could reveal bits of the genome that were shared among all those with the disease.

In the last four years, the search for disease genes has advanced again with the introduction of "next generation sequencing" which has enabled all 20,000 genes in the human genome to be sequenced for the same price as a single gene a decade ago. The new approach involves "dredging up everything in the sea" and using computer modelling to filter out what might be significant.

The technique yielded success in 2012 with the discovery of a new form of autosomal recessive skin EB caused – unexpectedly - by a mutation in the gene *exophilin 5* that controls the microtubal transport system in cells.

"The cause was so different from other forms of EB. Without next generation sequencing, this disease would have remained a mystery," said McGrath.

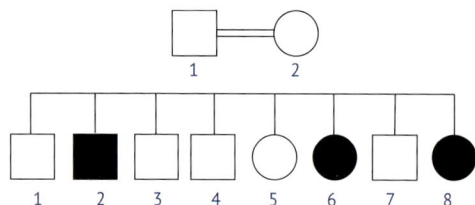

The family pedigree. Squares denote male family members, and circles female family members; filled-in symbols indicate clinically affected individuals.

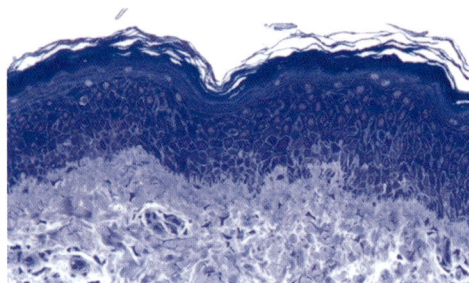

Light microscopy of skin reveals mild acanthosis and hyperkeratosis as well as a ruffled appearance to the dermal-epidermal junction (Richardson's stain; scale bar represents 50 μm).

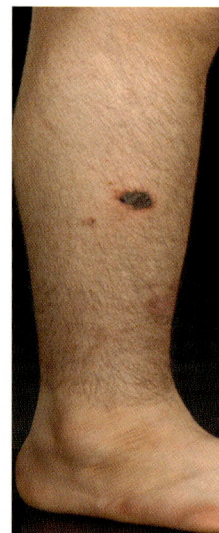

Affected individual II-2 with skin crusting at the site of a recent trauma-induced erosion.

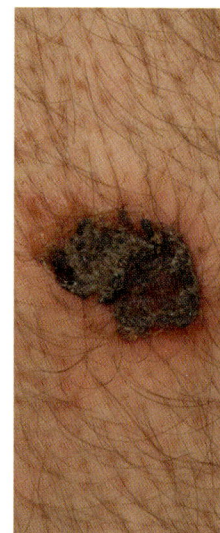

Higher magnification of the crusted erosion.

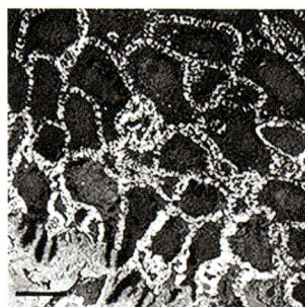

Low-magnification transmission electron micrograph shows widening of spaces between keratinocytes in the lower epidermis with some aggregation of keratin filaments (scale bar represents 3 μm).

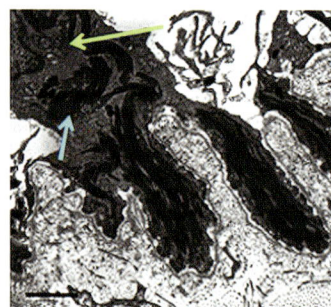

Higher-magnification transmission electron micrograph reveals keratin filament disruption (blue arrow) as well as perinuclear accumulation of vesicles (green arrow) (scale bar represents 0.5 μm).

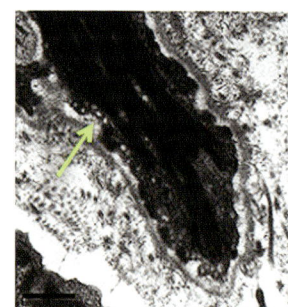

There is also focal accumulation of vesicles close to the plasma membrane (green arrow) (scale bar represents 0.25 μm).

Epidermolysis Bullosa

Imagine having skin that blistered at the slightest touch, that was so fragile a light knock could open a wound or a gentle rub leave it sore and bleeding. There are many different types and degrees of severity of the rare inherited skin disorder that affects an estimated 8,000 people in the UK and 500,000 worldwide. Around 420 of the most distressing cases are under the care of St John's.

Jemima Mellerio said: "It is a devastating disease. I can't think of any other condition where you are in pain every day of your life. It is not like something dreadful happens to you at age 10, say. It starts from birth, it is continuous every day, and it is your parents who are inflicting the pain, as they change your dressings. It affects the whole family."

It is not only the skin that is affected. Corneal blisters can appear on the eyes, the teeth may be affected, the oesophagus narrowed causing difficulty swallowing and other internal organs and membranes including the anus may be sore. Anaemia and constipation are the consequences.

The symptoms are caused by mutations in any of 18 different genes which make proteins that "stick" the top and bottom layer of skin together. There is no cure – doctors can only strive to minimise the effects. But that can mean the difference between a full life and half a one.

"Most of our patients are in mainstream school. We have young adults who are learning to drive, attending university, some have relationships, some have children. When you visit patients in other countries you realise: we do a lot," said Mellerio.

Until a decade ago the care delivered to EB

patients was haphazard, relying on the goodwill of the many specialties involved to give of their time and expertise. In 2002 the National Specialised Services Commissioning Group established St John's as one of four national centres for patients with EB (the others are at Great Ormond Street in London and Birmingham Children's Hospital and Heartlands Hospital in Birmingham). This meant, for the first time, there was a ring fenced pot of money to pay for the specialists required, ensuring a multidisciplinary approach. The National EB Diagnostic Laboratory is based at St John's providing analysis of skin biopsies, genetic testing

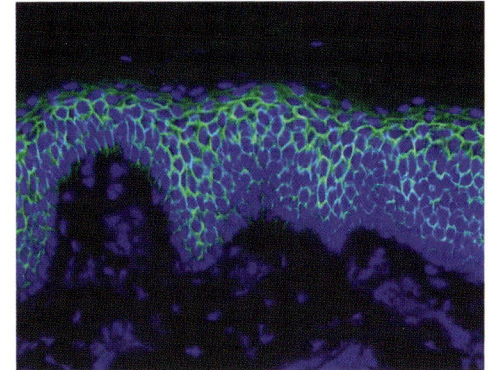

Immunofluorescence in Epidermolysis bullosa acquisita skin

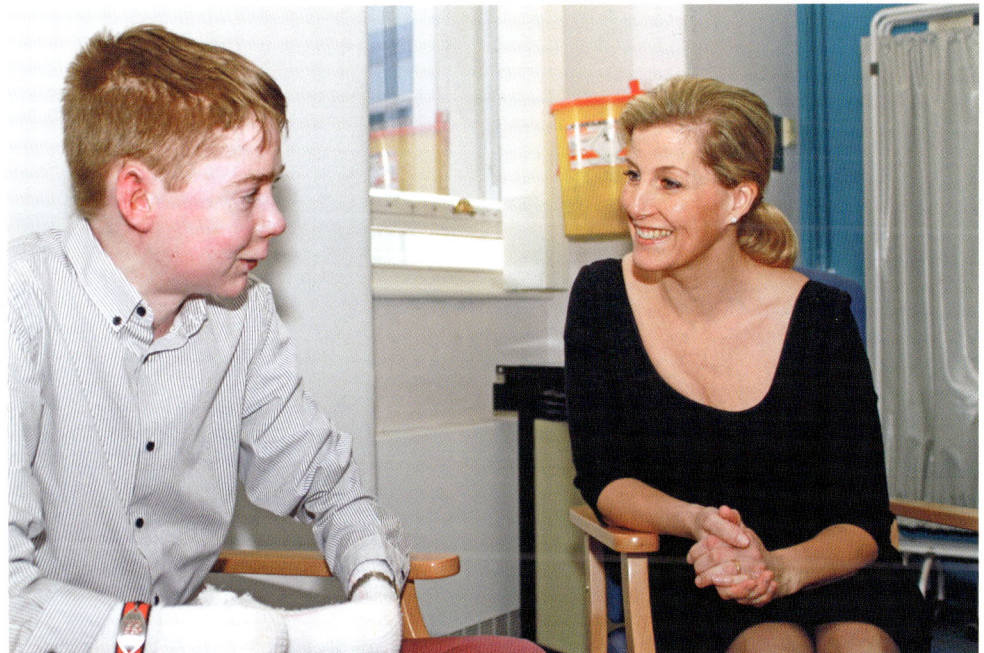

A patient with EB meets the Countess of Wessex. The condition causes blistering of the skin at the slightest touch

The National EB Diagnostic Laboratory is based at St John's providing analysis of skin biopsies, genetic testing and pre-natal diagnosis

and pre-natal diagnosis. A significant number of the St John's EB patients have severe disease and need services ranging from plastic surgery to palliative care.

The big threat to patients with severe EB is *squamous cell skin cancer*. Most start to develop it in their 20s, 30s and 40s but the youngest case was a child aged six, and there have been several in their early teens. It is a leading cause of death – Mellerio recalls a teenager who died aged 19 of the cancer.

"Patients tend to get one cancer, you cut it out and then another appears a year later. Then the disease accelerates. They face a lot of work cutting it out and having plastic surgery," she said.

For young people, on the cusp of adulthood this is hard news to absorb. They must be warned of the risk because they need to watch for changes in their skin and alert doctors when they notice one, so it can be biopsied. But information is shared on social networking sites – and some are terrified of what may happen.

"It is a sword hanging over them. It can be very difficult to manage. You jolly them along as kids but there is a real shift in their teens. I enjoy the transition – they can be infantilised in the children's department. But it is hard. Eventually they realise what they are facing – they vary enormously in their resilience. I quite like the stroppy teenagers – those with a certain strand of belligerence tend to do well."

"One patient said he had always thought having EB was like climbing a mountain. When he got his first cancer he realised that all the time he had just been in the foothills. He died as a young adult."

New Treatments

St John's is pioneering efforts to find new treatments for EB and other skin diseases. At least four trials were underway at the time of writing.

1 Stem cell therapy

One of the most exciting is an attempt to ease the impact of the disease by infusing bone marrow-derived stem cells from unmatched donors to create a generic anti-inflammatory effect. Ten children have been included in the trial which began in the autumn of 2013 and each has had three infusions of the mesenchymal stromal cells over 28 days into a vein. It is a small, Phase 1 trial to test the safety of the procedure. However, early results suggest the children have less pain, less itching, more appetite, more energy and their wounds heal faster. "We expect the effects to wear off but we may be able to do it again," said McGrath. The technique is also being tried in the Netherlands. The group at St John's also works closely with colleagues in the USA who are developing bone marrow transplantation for EB (the external advisory committee is chaired by Professor McGrath). Much work still needs to be done, however, before bone marrow transplantation can ever be considered a routine treatment for the clinic .

2 Fibroblasts

In this research, adults with EB have been injected with fibroblasts, the cells that produce collagen, to speed healing. The cells were injected around the edges of wounds and the results showed a statistically significant improvement in rates of healing for the first 28 days.. The study was published in the British Journal of Dermatology (October 2013). It is likely that more injections will be needed to heal most wounds. Injecting fibroblasts can be painful, and new devices are being developed to make the injections hurt less.

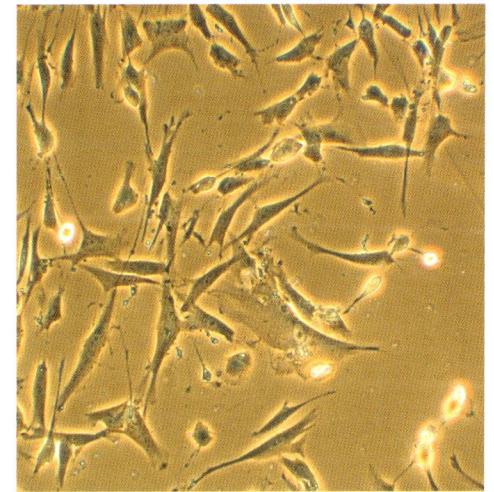

Human fibroblast cells – injected into EB patients to speed healing

3 Gene therapy

Clinical trials of correcting EB skin cells by replacing the responsible gene outside the body and then grafting them back is in progress in the USA and Europe, but the group at St John's is focusing on gene correction of the patient's own fibroblasts. "We have a lot of experience with injecting fibroblasts. Now we want to go to the next step of putting back the patient's own cells after we have corrected the gene. Hopefully this will lead to stronger skin that remains so for a long time," said McGrath.

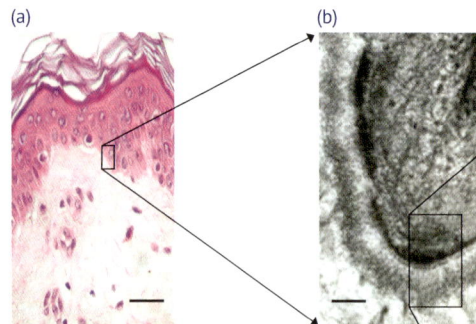

4 Natural gene therapy

One of the curiosities of EB is that some patients have areas of skin that never get blisters. The genes in those areas appear able to reboot themselves providing doctors with an opportunity to use the "healthy skin" to treat the "unhealthy" areas. By culturing keratinocytes – the outer skin cells – from the healthy tissue it should be possible to create skin grafts to repair the wounds. In the Netherlands, researchers have used punch-grafting in one patient – taking small pieces of the healthy skin and seeding them in areas of unhealthy skin – with good early results.

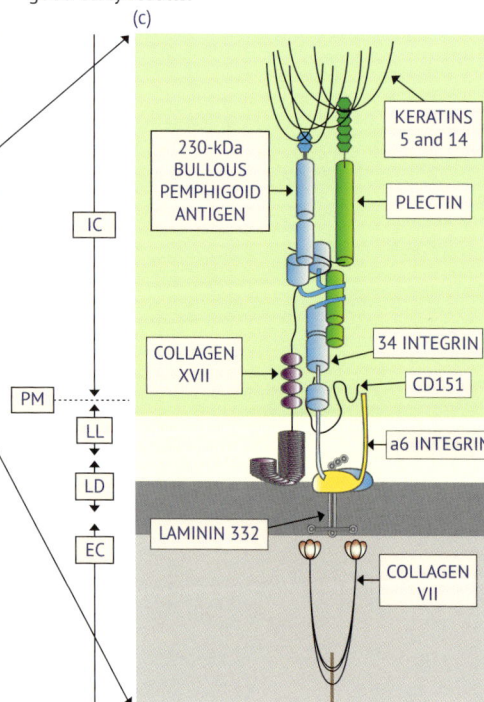

5 Inducible pluripotent stem cell therapy

One of the most significant advances of the last seven years has been the discovery that an ordinary skin cell can be re-programmed to behave like an embryonic stem cell and develop into any tissue in the body. The technique has so far been used on keratinocytes taken from healthy patches of skin on EB patients, which have been programmed to form skin progenitor cells which could be used for treating EB. Because they are the patient's own cells rather than provided by a donor there is no risk of rejection. In patients who lack healthy patches of

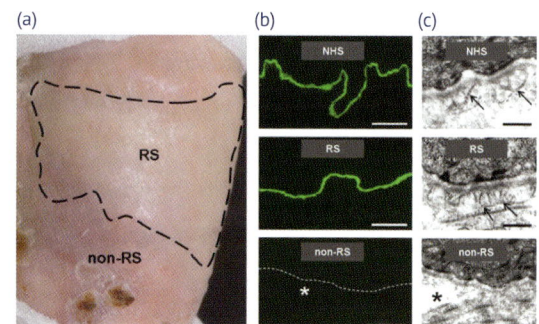

(a) (b)

The molecular basis of inherited skin blistering involving hemidesmosome-associated proteins. (a) Light microscopy image of the skin; the boxed area indicates a dermal-epidermal junction (b) Transmission electron microscopy image of a dermal-epidermal junction; hemidesmosome attachment complexes are boxed (scale bar=0.1 μm); (c) A schematic representation of the protein organization of dermal-epidermal attachment complexes, the intrinsic proteins and the genes encoding them, and the associated genetic diseases. Revertant mosaicism has been reported for keratin 14 (KRT14), laminin-332 (LAMB3), type XVII collagen (COL17A1) and type VII collagen (COL7A1).

(c)

KERATINS 5 and 14

230-kDa BULLOUS PEMPHIGOID ANTIGEN

PLECTIN

IC

COLLAGEN XVII

β4 INTEGRIN

CD151

PM

α6 INTEGRIN

LL

LD

LAMININ 332

EC

COLLAGEN VII

(a) (b) (c)

NHS NHS

RS RS

non-RS non-RS

RS

non-RS

Revertant mosaicism in RDEB. (a) Clinical evidence of reverted (RS) and unreverted (nonRS) skin; note the severe blistering phenotype in the nonRS area. (b) Immunofluorescence image showing Type VII collagen expression shows bright linear labeling at the dermal-epidermal junction in normal human skin (NHS) and in the RS but no signal is detected in the nonRS sample (dashed line indicates dermal-epidermal junction; asterisk depicts subepidermal blistering, scale bar=50 μm). (c) Transmission electron microscopy images showing anchoring fibrils beneath the lamina densa in NHS and also in RS (arrows) but not in nonRS samples. There is also blistering beneath the lamina densa in nonRS sample (asterisk). Scale bar=0.2 μm

skin, the researchers plan to use gene editing techniques to correct the genetic fault. Writing in the Journal of Investigative Dermatology (January 2014) the authors, including McGrath from St John's, say the approach should be "the starting point for autologous [from the same body] cellular therapies using natural gene therapy" in EB.

Other research is assessing the potential of protein and drug therapy. As many of the severely affected EB patients lack collagen VII, essential for maintaining the structure of the skin, one approach is to replace it directly. Micro-needles, no bigger than the mouth parts of a mosquito, are coated with collagen VII and stuck through the skin in the hope that the collagen will dissolve off directly into the cells, helping the inner and outer layers of the skin to stick together. If the technique proves effective the collagen could be delivered by a dressing covered with fine needles that have first been coated with it. Research is also underway to give replacement protein therapy by intravenous injection - in France, experiments with this approach have been carried out on dogs.

Drugs are being developed to repair some types of genetic mutation, and have been trialled in *muscular dystrophy* and *cystic fibrosis*. If successful they may be extended to include EB.

McGrath said: "St Johns is not about treating conditions seen at the local district hospital. This is where the buck stops. We are here for patients who can't be treated anywhere else."

"I joined the Institute in the 1990s and have had a couple of decades making discoveries. Now I want to give something back to the patients – designing and carrying out clinical trials of new therapies. That is going to be my work for the next decade."

The Autologous Transplant Process

1. Collection
Stem cells are collected from the patient's bone marrow or blood.

2. Processing
Blood or bone marrow is processed in the laboratory to purify and concentrate the stem cell.

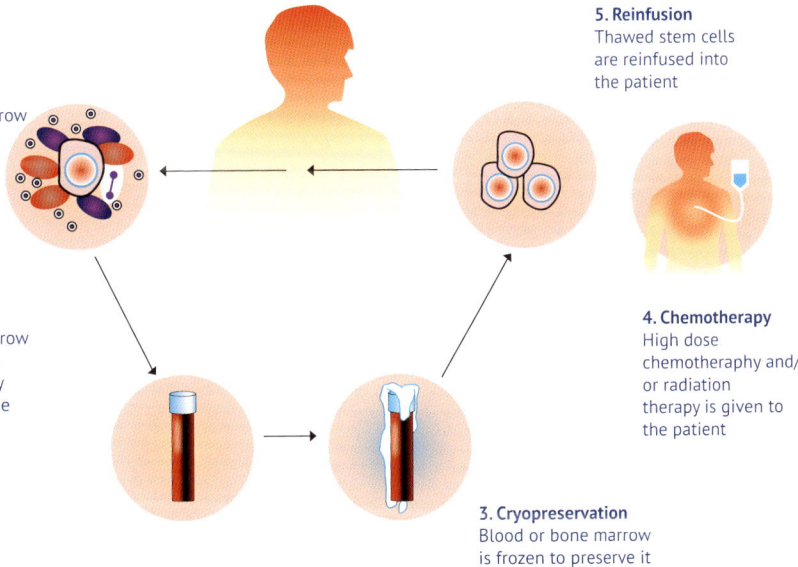

3. Cryopreservation
Blood or bone marrow is frozen to preserve it

4. Chemotherapy
High dose chemotheraphy and/ or radiation therapy is given to the patient

5. Reinfusion
Thawed stem cells are reinfused into the patient

The autologous transplant process – removing stem cells from a patient before treatment with high dose chemotherapy, then replacing them afterwards

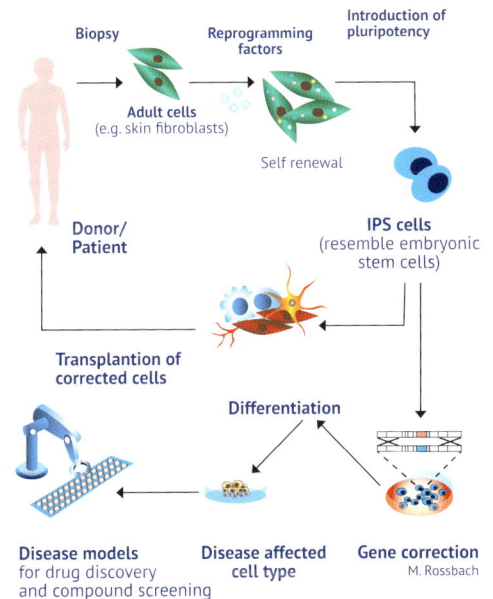

Biopsy

Reprogramming factors

Introduction of pluripotency

Adult cells
(e.g. skin fibroblasts)

Self renewal

Donor/ Patient

IPS cells
(resemble embryonic stem cells)

Transplantion of corrected cells

Differentiation

Disease models
for drug discovery and compound screening

Disease affected cell type

Gene correction
M. Rossbach

Induce pluripotent stem cell therapy – re-programming skin cells to become stem cells

Nursing

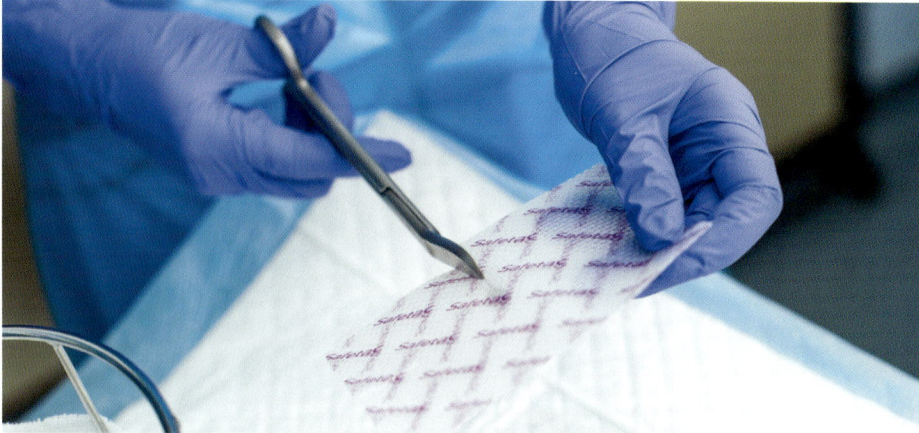

Dressings have advanced from traditional gauzes to soft silicone and there are a range of garments, including tubular vests and leggings to hold them in place.

Caring for people with EB who have fragile, blistering skin is extremely challenging. St John's has five specialist nurses who go out into the community to help adult EB patients and their families in their own homes, advising about skin care, liaising with employers or university/colleges and educating local nurses. They also provide end of life care to patients with advanced cancer related to their EB.

In the past they were funded by DEBRA, the national charity for people with EB, but are now funded 75 per cent by the NHS.

Separately, Great Ormond Street provides specially trained nurses to support families with EB. When notified of the birth of an affected baby they will give advice to the local nurses caring for it over the phone and make home visits to the family throughout childhood.

"Within 24 to 48 hours one of the Great Ormond Street nurses will travel anywhere in the country to take skin biopsies and blood for genetic testing. They will advise nurses about putting babygros on inside out, so the seams don't rub, and avoiding plastic name tags. They will also take dressings and give advice on feeding," said Mellerio.

Dressings have advanced from traditional bandages and gauzes pre-1990 to Vaseline gauze in the mid-1990s to soft silicone dressings post-2000.

Today nurses have developed a range of garments, including tubular vests and leggings to hold the dressings in place.

Mellerio said: "If you have a baby with severe ichthyosis and the nurses on the neo-natal ward have no expertise, it is hard. I would like to see a community outreach service introduced for other skin diseases."

CASE STUDY - BETHAN THOMAS

Every eight weeks or so Bethan Thomas has to return to St Thomas' from her home in South Wales to have her oesophagus dilated – a challenging procedure that requires several days in hospital.

"They can never predict how long because nothing ever goes smoothly with me," she says with a shrug.

She is 37 and a lifelong sufferer from *recessive dystrophic EB of an unusual type – inversa*. She has a badly affected mouth with a narrow opening, a tied tongue, blisters on the inside of her cheeks and difficulty swallowing and eating. In addition to the regular dilatations of her oesophagus, she has a feeding tube direct into her stomach.

Despite these difficulties she has never let her illness stop her doing what she wanted. "My parents never treated me any different to my brother. I wasn't molly coddled. If they said I couldn't do it, I did it anyway."

A self confessed tomboy, she played rugby as a teenager, hung out with the lads and discovered alcohol. "I was never in. I was always out with the boys. I worked in a pub. I'm not scared of nothing."

Her truculence has served her well. Today she lives with her partner, Badyn, 42, a window maker, and her teenage daughter, Georgia, who is taking her GCSEs.

"I know people who let EB rule their life. When Georgia was born they said come and have it in St Thomas'. I said no child of mine is going to be born in England." She had a planned Caesarean in her local district hospital instead.

She has had a number of crises, including several spells in hospital for *septicaemia*. Blue light ambulances have rushed her through the streets. "It's my oesophagus that's knackered. But if you can't swallow you panic and then you can't breathe."

She tries to do without her feeding tube, drinking up to 16 pints of milk a week. Solid food is more challenging – it may take her two hours to eat a sandwich.

"I have managed for 37 years. I don't know how I do it but I do. My throat hurts a lot but I can't do nothing about it. That's life."

She has stopped coming for out patient appointments . "I'm not coming all the way to London for half an hour. They know me – I don't bother them unless I need to. If I ring they know there is something wrong. I have seen enough doctors."

She tries not to think about the future. She knows there is a risk of cancer. But anyone can get it, she says. "It is always in the back of my mind. But if you start thinking that way you might as well just curl up."

CASE STUDY - **MANDY ALDWIN**

The unpredictability of her condition is the hardest part for Mandy Aldwin. She has ichthyosis of a rare type called Netherton syndrome which causes reddened scaling skin, with her face being most severely affected. It is an inherited condition that can be managed but it can't be cured.

"Unlike psoriasis and eczema, it's not patchy but affects all of my skin all of the time. I manage it with a daily regime of creams and lotions. My type flares up and I get infections so I have to take antibiotics. It's on and off sore most days – but it can be extremely painful and then I have to rest. The best treatment, apart from a lot of grease and emollients, is bed rest."

Now aged 37, she was cared for at Great Ormond Street as a child because her local hospital in Reading did not know how to cope. On reaching the age of 16 and becoming an adult she was discharged but four years later she had a crisis at the age of 20.

"My skin suddenly deteriorated. There was a major change in the way it was behaving. My skin was very bad and did not get better – it went on for months."

Her mother was desperate for help and called St John's for advice. Mandy was admitted to a bed in St Thomas' and remained in hospital for over two weeks.

That was 17 years ago. She has been under the care of the Genetics department at St John's ever since and attends the hospital every six months for a check.

"I can contact them when I need to. But under their guidance I am self managing now. I know what to do – I just refer to them for reassurance and any new information."

"Other people's reactions were hurtful as a child."

Coping with the condition is not just a matter of managing the physical symptoms. Like all skin ailments, it has a psychological impact too. "My skin is very inflamed and peels. Other people's reactions leave something to be desired. It comes down to a lack of knowledge – but it was hurtful as a child. To a certain extent I have learnt to deal with it, but if it looks particularly bad I might decide I do not want to go and do the food shop."

Mandy and her mother, Maggie are two of the founder trustees of the Ichthyosis Support Group which now has 600 members across the country. Sharing experiences helps, she said, and the group also helps focus efforts to improve treatment and care.

"The attitude of doctors has changed. My consultant, Jemima Mellerio, is very empathetic and appreciates the person behind the condition. In earlier years, consultants were very much focused on the condition. It is so much better, psychologically, to be treated as a person than as a fascinating condition."

THE SUN: ITS DANGERS AND HEALING POWER

Monthly Average UV - Index

Low temperature → High temperature ← Low temperature

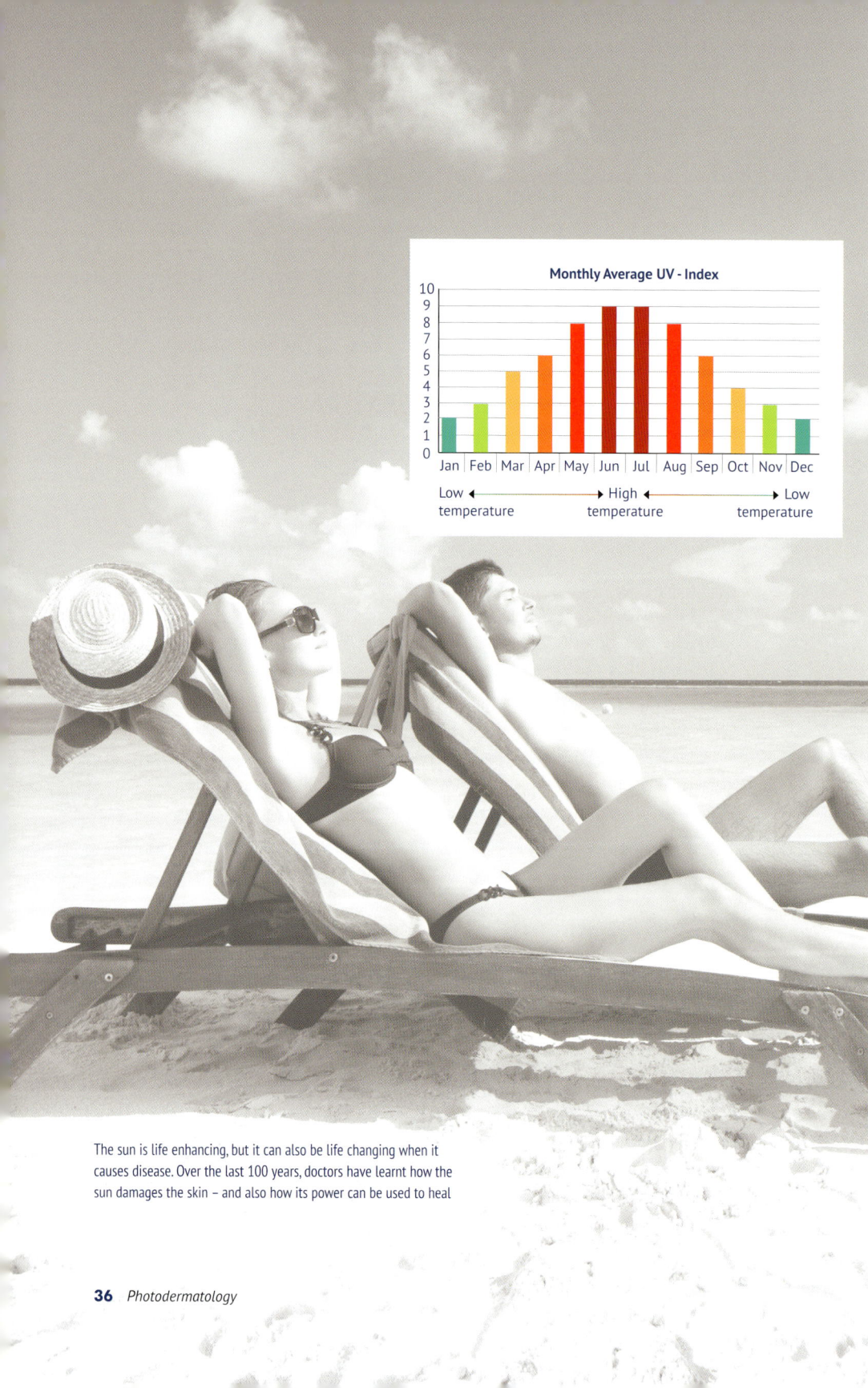

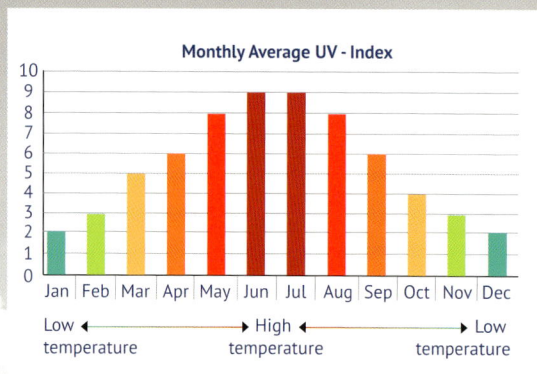

Few things are more life enhancing than the sight of the sun. We worship it in summer, long for it in winter, and spend large sums of money chasing it round the globe.

But it is also damaging. Nothing ages the skin faster than the sun. People who spend days exposed to it – from Australian sheep farmers to Californian ladies who lunch – have the prematurely wrinkled faces to prove it.

We all benefit and we are all, to some degree, at risk. But for a few unlucky individuals the sun poses a more serious threat. They come out in lumps and rashes, their skin itches and burns and they may experience screaming pain after even brief exposure. Some will develop skin cancer in early adulthood and die.

Over the last 100 years, doctors have learnt how the sun damages the skin, who is most vulnerable and how best to protect them. In doing so they have also learnt how to use its properties to heal. They have harnessed the power of the sun.

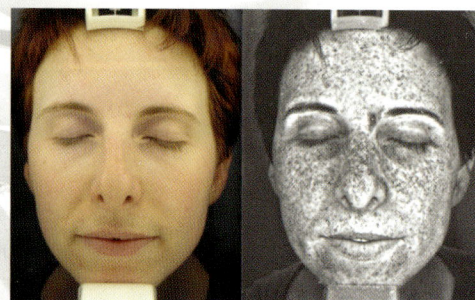

Ultraviolet imaging demonstrates sun damage in a melanoma patient

The sun is life enhancing, but it can also be life changing when it causes disease. Over the last 100 years, doctors have learnt how the sun damages the skin – and also how its power can be used to heal

History

Nobel prizewinner Niels Finsen, inventor of the first sun lamp

Researchers began investigating sunburn in the mid-19th century. At first it was thought that heat from the sun was responsible until it became clear that , in fact, it was the ultra violet component causing the damage. Ultraviolet radiation (UVR) had previously been identified from its effect on silver chloride paper, the forerunner of photographic film.

In 1903 **Niels Finsen** of Denmark was awarded the Nobel prize for producing the world's first sun lamp to create UVR which he used to treat *tuberculosis of the skin*. Over the subsequent decades, UVR was used as a therapy for a range of other conditions, including *psoriasis*.

But while UVR therapy developed, the diagnosis and treatment of people with extreme sunlight sensitivity stalled. Although some conditions had been known about for a long time, there was no systematic attempt to investigate them until the development of phototesting at St John's Institute of Dermatology in the 1950s.

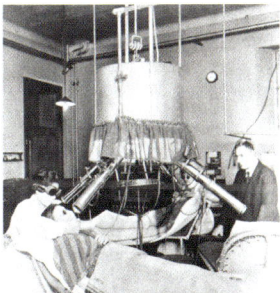

Finsen lamp treatment, London 1925

Photodermatoses

These are diseases caused by sensitivity to sunlight, which contains two sorts of ultraviolet radiation – UVA and B (a third sort, UVC, is absorbed by the atmosphere and does not reach the Earth). They include the very common *polymorphic light eruption* (prickly heat), characterised by rashes on the skin following sun exposure, affecting one in six people, mostly women (St John's sees only the severest cases); *chronic actinic dermatitis* (light sensitive eczema), one of the commonest forms of severe eczema, which can be triggered by tiny amounts of sun light; and *actinic prurigo*, which affects children causing itchy rashes that may last for months after a single exposure.

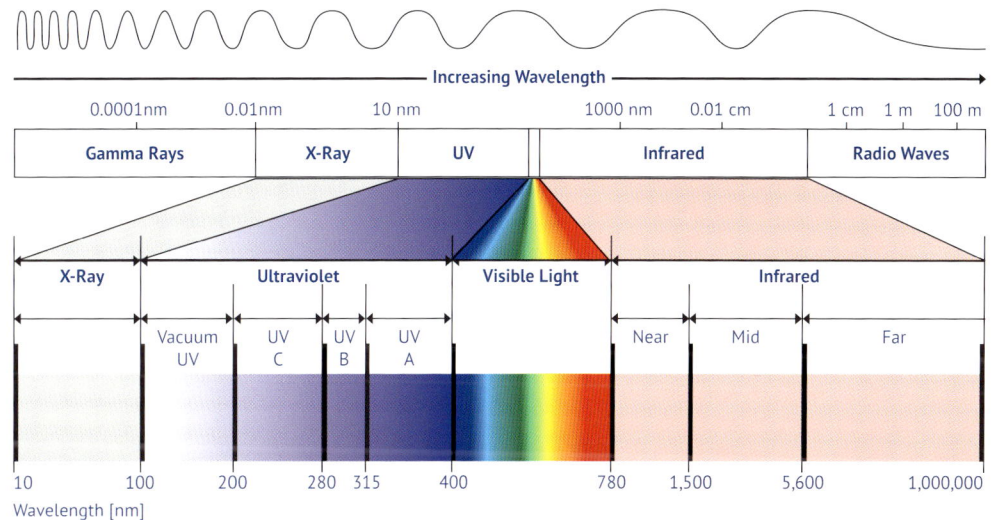

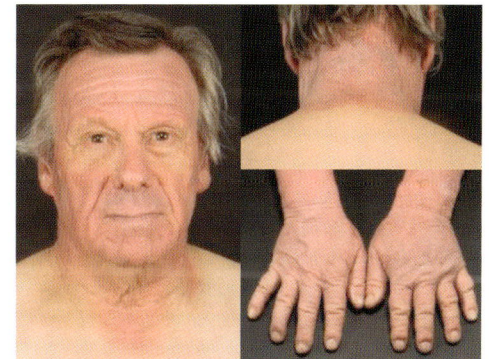

Patient with chronic actinic dermatitis caused by sunlight

In all these cases, the first requirement is an accurate diagnosis. A severe eczema on the face could be caused by a cream, or allergy to sunlight. Phototesting is crucial to determine if sensitivity to sunlight is the cause.

St John's became the first institution in the world to introduce phototesting using a machine designed by **Ian Magnus**, a consultant dermatologist and pioneer in clinical and experimental photobiology who created phototesting at the Institute in 1953.

It worked on the same principle as patch testing for allergies. Magnus' machine, called a monochromator, produced UVR of different wavelengths which was focused on a grid placed across the patient's back and delivered at a variety of doses and wavelengths to the skin. The strength of the reaction indicated the sensitivity of the skin to that particular wavelength. Specific patterns of sensitivity were found to correlate with specific clinical diseases, so the approach enabled accurate diagnosis of photosensitive skin diseases for the first time. In addition, phototesting could identify whether UVA or UVB was responsible and thus which sunscreen and other photoprotection to recommend.

Patients were referred to Magnus's clinic from all over South England. The Photobiology unit was established by Magnus and **Arthur Porter** and later developed through the 1980s and 1990s by Professors **John Hawk** and **Anthony Young**. St John's still has the largest clinical service for photosensitivity, and the largest phototesting service in England and one of the largest in the world, and the monochromator remains the key diagnostic tool.

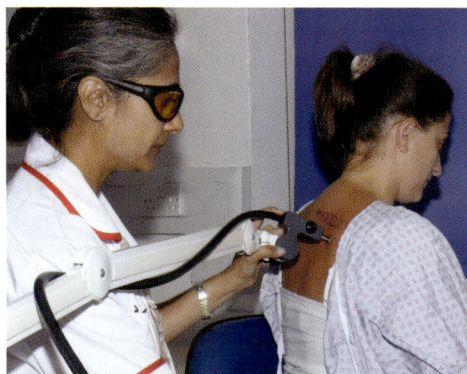

Phototesting using the monochromator – St John's was the first institution in the world to introduce phototesting

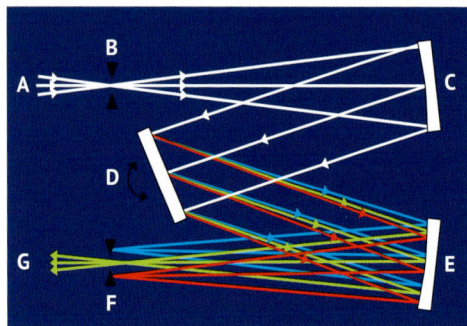

Ultraviolet radiation is separated into individual wavelengths with the monochromator

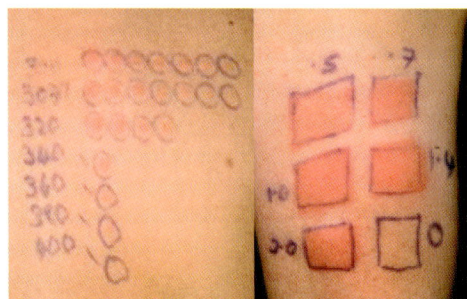

Positive phototests in a patient with chronic actinic dermatitis

Accurate diagnosis leads to appropriate treatment. Adults and Children with severe and treatment resistant *actinic prurigo* can be treated with thalidomide, the drug that caused a scandal in the 1960s when it was prescribed to pregnant women for morning sickness and led to the birth of thousands of malformed babies. As a treatment for *actinic prurigo* it can be used safely and effectively – the itchy rashes in the skin just melt away.

Polymorphic light eruption (prickly heat) can be treated prophylactically with gentle tanning under a UVB lamp in the spring. This hardens the skin and desensitises the immune system so it calms down when exposed to UVR in summer sunshine.

Phototherapy

Every time a person goes outside, UVR from the sun is absorbed by their skin causing damage to the cells that make it grow and function correctly. In sensitive people the immune system reacts causing inflammation, leading to the pimples and rashes characteristic of a flare.

But in others, exposure to sunlight can ease skin conditions by calming the immune system down and reducing inflammation. This explains why teenagers with acne often find their skin improves in summer with exposure to the sun.

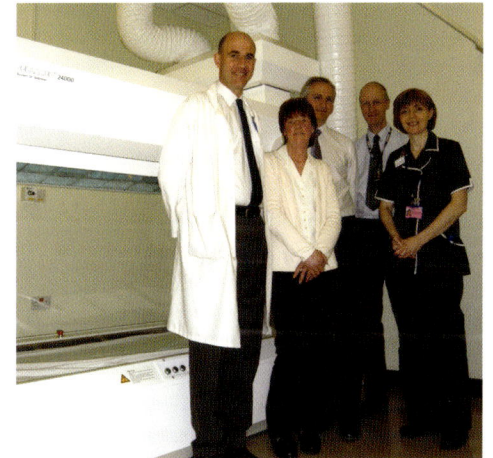

The first patient to be treated with the UVA1 machine in 2007 (second left) with staff from St John's

The therapeutic effect of UV light, discovered by Nobel prize winning Neils Finsen, is harnessed today by exposing the skin to it in the form of UVB phototherapy or with UVA in combination with psoralens (PUVA), natural compounds known to the ancient Egyptians for sensitising the skin to the sun, whose efficacy was rediscovered in the 1950s.

Ultraviolet radiation from the sun causes damage to skin cells – but it can also ease skin conditions by calming the immune system down and reducing inflammation

PUVA phototherapy involves applying a cream to the skin or taking a tablet containing psoralens and then exposing the skin to UVA. PUVA treatment is especially used at St John's to treat *cutaneous lymphoma*, as well as a variety of other diseases particularly when UVB therapy has not been effective.

Vitiligo is a particular problem in black and Asian communities where white patches on the skin are much more noticeable. It is caused by the immune system attacking the skin cells which produce melanin, the pigment that gives the skin its colour. It is often dismissed as a cosmetic problem – but it can be devastating. Steroid creams are often tried and when they fail prolonged courses of UVB phototherapy can be effective in many patients.

The phototherapy unit at St John's is a national centre for phototherapy and acts as the hub for support and training of a network of phototherapy units in hospitals throughout South East England. In addition to the usual range of treatments it is one of only three centres in Britain (the others are in Leeds and Dundee) providing high output UVA1 therapy (shown in photo on previous page). This is a treatment introduced at St John's in 2007 for diseases such as *scleroderma*, which causes fibrosis of the skin, and *graft vs host disease* that can follow bone marrow transplantation making the skin woody and hard.

The long wave UVR is delivered in large doses by a room-sized machine that generates a lot of heat and must be cooled by powerful fans. It is particularly effective against skin diseases where there is extensive scarring, thickening or stiffening of the skin.

One of the dangers of phototherapy is accidental overdose, causing burns and increasing the risk of skin cancer. It is the single largest cause of successful litigation in dermatology. Since 2008, St John's has led a programme in the south east England clinical network to educate nurses in how to give patients phototherapy safely and to monitor treatment in the region. Evidence shows that standards have improved with patients' conditions better managed and a safer and more effective service.

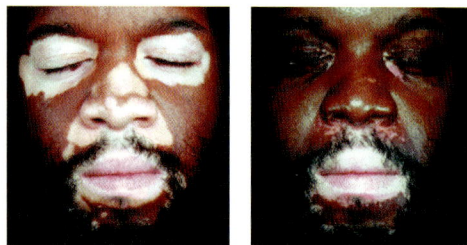

A patient with vitiligo before and after treatment with phototherapy. Vitiligo is caused by the immune system attacking melanin-producing skin cells

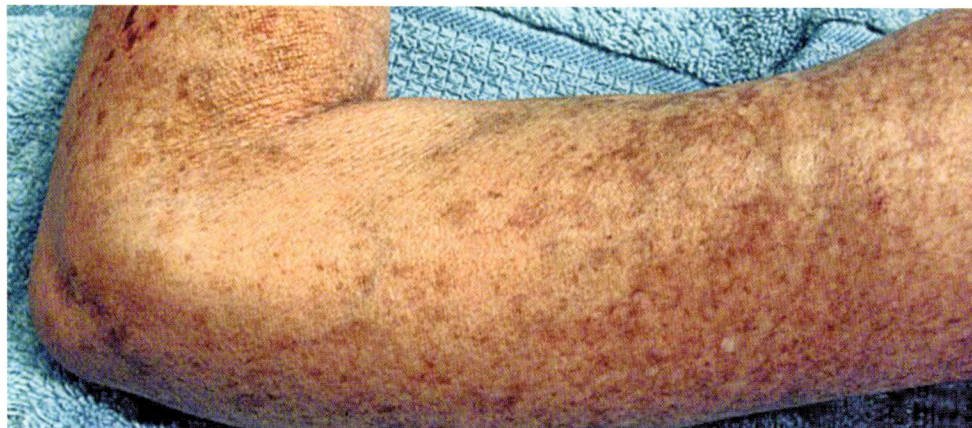

A case of scleroderma: UVA1 phototherapy

Porphyria

A rare and severe group of skin diseases – the *cutaneous porphyrias*, are caused by the build up of porphyrins in the skin. The name refers to a group of conditions resulting from inherited enzyme disorders.

Porphyria is derived from the Greek meaning "purple pigment" on account of the dark colour of urine and faeces in some affected individuals. Under normal circumstances porphyrins are converted to heme, a precursor of haemoglobin, the constituent of red blood cells that carries oxygen round the body. But when the process breaks down and the porphyrins build up, sufferers become sensitive to sunlight.

In *erythropoietic protoporphyria (EPP)*, patients experience intense burning and swelling of the skin when exposed to the sun, complaining that their hands and face feel on fire with attacks lasting several days. Ian Magnus of St John's played a key role in describing EPP. Although there had

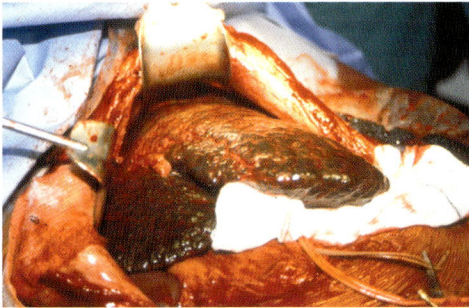

A cirrhotic liver caused by erythropoietic protoporphyria. Sun exposure leads to the build up of toxic porphyrins which can result in liver failure requiring a liver transplant

been a hint that *porphyrins* were involved in the condition he was able to confirm that the pain and swelling sufferers experienced when exposed to the sun was indeed due to the build up of porphyrins to toxic levels in their skin.

As shown in the figure above EPP occasionally also causes liver failure requiring a liver transplant.

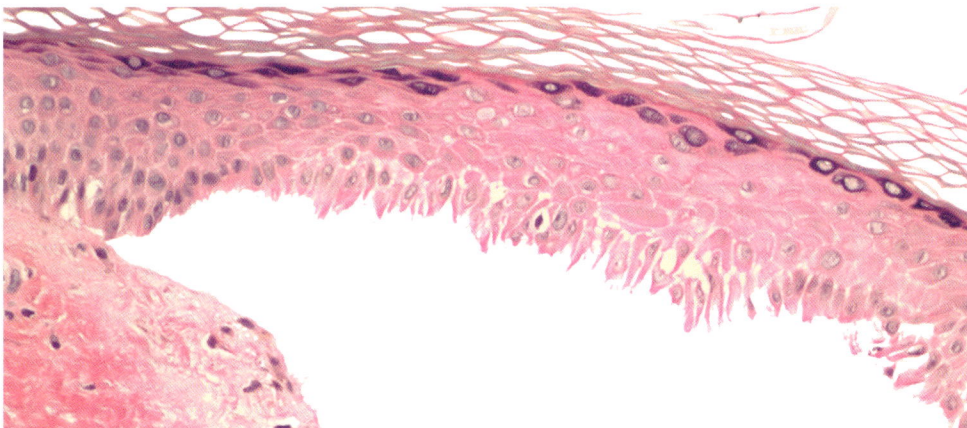

Porphyria cutanea tarda: skin histology shows the split in the dermis where the disease has caused blistering

The rarest type of *cutaneous porphyria* is *Gunther's disease*, a congenital condition which is very severe, involving extreme photosensitivity, brown teeth that fluoresce in ultraviolet light and purple body fluid. Other effects include severe blistering and scarring of the eyes and fingers, increased hair growth on the forehead, and potentially fatal effects in the blood. Gunther's disease is severe and disabling and some patients who are severely affected may be unable to go outside during the day. It is possible that Gunther's disease has led in primitive societies to various legends involving vampires and werewolves. Such responses illustrate graphically how severe photosensitivity is not only disabling but has the potential to be deeply stigmatising too.

Today St John's is one of the main centres for the treatment of *cutaneous porphyrias*, seeing around 80 of the 230 patients in the country and around half of the 20 patients with Gunther's disease.

Xeroderma Pigmentosum

This rare, hereditary disorder, affecting one in 250,000 people, highlights the devastating effect the sun can have. Sufferers are unable to repair the damage caused by UVR present in sunlight, even in winter, putting them at exceptionally high risk of developing skin cancer. Diagnosis often follows severe and exaggerated sunburn when the child is first exposed to sunlight.

St John's provides the largest multidisciplinary clinical service for XP in the world, and the only expert centre in the UK, treating 80 of the 90-100 patients with the condition in the country. It is unique in providing psychological cover – living in fear of the sun creates immense pressure on the whole family – and outreach nurses who visit patients' homes and schools to check on UVR exposure and advise on protective measures.

XP, an autosomal recessive gene disorder, is often marked by the development of hundreds of 'freckles' at an early age. Other symptoms include dry skin, blistering on slightest sun exposure, patches of rough skin (solar keratoses) and painfully sun sensitive eyes that may become bloodshot and clouded.

As with *porphyria*, sun avoidance is crucial to maintaining the health of patients with XP. The first inkling of the condition may come when a mother turns up at A&E with a severely sunburnt child, and is often scolded for leaving it in the sun. Yet just five minutes exposure may result in very severe and exaggerated sunburn with blistering.

Sun avoidance involves elaborate protection, with gloves, hats and UVR-protective visors whenever sufferers venture outside. Windows at home, school and in the car must be covered with

A researcher working on Xeroderma Pigmentosum, which affects one in 250,000 people leaving them unable to repair the skin damage caused by the sun, even in winter

UVR-filter film to prevent inadvertent exposure through the glass.

The risk of cancer is ever present. **Robert Sarkany**, head of the photodermatology department, said: "I saw a girl who had her first skin cancer when she was six, despite being dark-skinned. Another patient had had 150 skin cancers cut out by the age of 35. The most common cause of death in these patients is *melanoma* and the mean lifespan is 32. They can also get eye cancer and go blind. On top of that around 30 per cent develop neurological complications. It is a dreadful disease."

The multiplicity of XP patients' needs meant they could not be met by dermatologists alone. When Dr Sarkany joined St John's in 2006 he saw the need for a multidisciplinary service. Drawing on his previous experience with a trial specialist XP service in Worthing, he worked with the patient support group led by **Sandra Webb**, mother of 16 year old Alex, a sufferer, to design a more effective service.

"Our most severely ill patients had needs we were not meeting. There was lots of skin cancer, eye damage, 'freckling' that we were not dealing with. The patient support group was pretty angry. We had to do something better," he said.

In 2008, he started a specialist XP clinic, with ophthalmologists and neurologists, held three times a year. Two years later in 2010 it was launched as a separate national XP service funded by the Department of Health, providing a multidisciplinary clinic fortnightly, headed by consultant dermatologist **Hiva Fassihi**.

The clinic treats adults and children from across the UK working with specialists in photodermatology, dermatological surgery, plastic

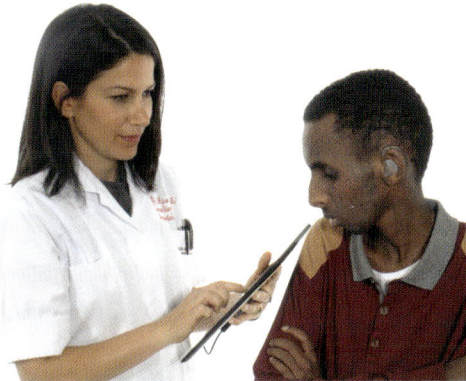

Hiva Fassihi (Clinical Lead of the UK National XP Service) with an XP patient

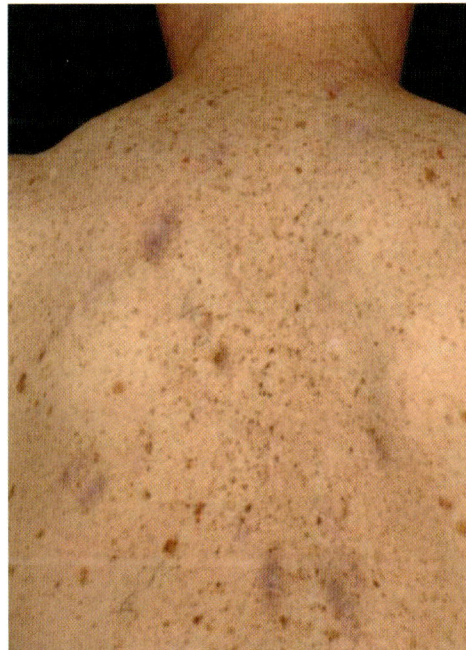

Patient with multiple scars from skin cancer surgery

surgery, genetics, neurology, ophthalmology and psychology. It is the only clinic in the world that looks after patients long term, at the hospital and in their home environment.

Among the specialists it calls on are those in the dermatological surgery department working with the laser scanning confocal microscope, the only one of its kind in the NHS. The microscope allows suspicious skin lesions to be scanned and assessed at a cellular level, thereby avoiding the unnecessary excision of lesions that turn out to be benign (see Chapter 4).

The service's holistic approach is illustrated by the outreach work of the clinic's specialist nurses which was recently assessed. The results showed that in over 90 per cent of the 20 schools visited, where advice had been given about improving protection by putting UVR-filter film on windows, UVR levels measured three months later had declined by at least 70 per cent. "We are the only unit to look after our patients in this fashion," said Dr Sarkany.

Research breakthrough in X-P

In addition to running the clinical service, the photodermatology department at St John's is undertaking cutting edge research. In 2013, they made a breakthrough in understanding of XP with the discovery that half of patients with the condition don't get abnormal and exaggerated sunburn from the sun.

As severe sunburn from minimal sun exposure has traditionally been thought to be a defining symptom of the disease, the discovery is of major clinical significance. The study, led by Hiva Fassihi and published in the British Journal of Dermatology, divided patients into eight groups and found their symptoms varied.

Those that did not suffer sunburn instead developed 'freckles' but were still more likely to develop cancer. The danger from believing that severe sunburn was the defining characteristic of the disease was that these patients (and/or their parents) might not bother with sun protection, exposing them to a higher risk of cancer.

Dr Fassihi said: "If you see a child who is becoming more and more 'freckly' you should think about XP, even if they don't sunburn."

Dr Sarkany said: "We are worried GPs, nurses and A&E staff may not know this. It is an important finding."

In addition to research at the cellular level, identifying which patients burn in the sun, doctors at St John's are also studying the impact of the illness on the psychological well being of the patient and their family. With the help of **John Weinman**, professor of psychology at Kings College, London, researchers are examining what effect having to hide from the sun, put on protective clothing each time they go out and live behind a visor are having on the individuals and their loved ones.

"If you wear a hood with a visor all the time you lead a very different, more isolated life compared with the rest of us. But if you don't, you get cancer. The question we are trying to answer is: 'What is it like to have this disease'".

A third avenue of research is provided by the overlap between *XP* and *Cockayne syndrome*, which causes premature ageing in children and involves failure in the same DNA repair pathway. Instead of skin cancers, Cockayne patients develop neurological problems as a result of the failed development of the nervous system.

A new national service is being established for Cockayne's patients based in the Clinical Genetics department of Guy's and St Thomas' headed by **Dr Shehla Mohammed**.

"We hope the two national services will provide extra insights working alongside each other," said Dr Sarkany.

CASE STUDY - **EDDISON MILLER**

The first sign that something was wrong with Eddison appeared when he was three months old. His parents Andrew, 37, a police officer and Nicola, 36, an architectural technologist, of Ashford, Kent, had taken him for a visit to some neighbours.

"Afterwards we noticed his face was red. It looked like a chemical burn. He had only been outside for a few minutes and I thought it must be a reaction to the suncream," said Nicola.

They took Eddison to the GP who told them it was probably eczema. This was the first of several visits to doctors triggered by Eddison's apparently hyper-sensitive reaction to being outside.

"They would say: 'It looks like sunburn.' We would reply: 'But he has hardly been outside.' They would look at us sceptically and say: 'Babies are sensitive.' We would respond: 'We know.'"

"It got to the point where we were not being listened to. So, on our GP's suggestion, we went private."

The consultant dermatologist they saw could not diagnose Eddison's condition, instead referring the family to John's. There a biopsy was taken of Eddison's skin and two months later the family was asked back to be given the findings.

"That was when we were told he had *Xeroderma Pigmentosum* – which is incredibly rare. Right up to that point I assumed it was an allergy. The paediatric nurse took Eddison off to play while Hiva Fassihi, the consultant, explained what it meant and how we would have to reconfigure our lives. It was a massive shock –

Eddison Miller, age 3, in his UVR- protective clothing and (below) his "indoor garden". Even the 40 watt light bulb was too strong and had to be changed

but the care we have had has been absolutely fantastic," said Nicola.

Eddison was then 13 months old. From that day his routine changed. To protect him from UV radiation he has Factor 50 suncream applied every three hours and must wear full body, head and face cover, including gloves. At home all the windows have been covered with a special film that filters out UVA and UVB radiation. Even the light bulbs had to be changed – any over 40 watts had to go and halogen spotlights had to be replaced with LEDs.

Now aged three, going out in his full protective gear is a trial. He gets hot and dehydrated, it is difficult to hear and when windy his visor gets pressed against his face.

On one occasion, the family – there is also a younger brother, Raife, who is unaffected – went for an outing to the beach by moonlight so Eddison could run around without his protetive clothing. But the sensation of sand between his toes and wind in his hair was overwhelming. "We underestimated

Eddison will need regular medical checks for the rest of his life

how much of a sensory overload it would be," said Nicola.

She and Andrew launched an appeal for funds to build an "indoor garden", which was completed in Autumn 2013, where he can now play with friends.

He will shortly start at nursery school where staff have been specially trained to deal with his particular needs. At St John's, which he attends regularly for check ups by a multidisciplinary team, doctors are so pleased with his progress they have said he does not need to return for a year.

Nicola said: "Developmentally and mentally he is doing really well. If anything he is ahead of his peers. His stamina has improved enormously since he had the indoor garden."

The future is uncertain and he will need regular medical checks for the rest of his life to detect any sign of cancer or neurological problems. But for now things are looking rosy for the boy who is one in a quarter million.

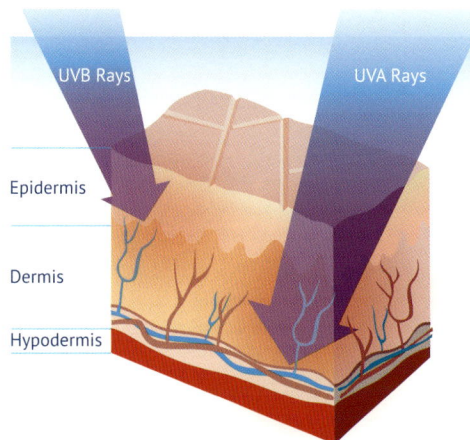

UVB Rays   UVA Rays

Epidermis

Dermis

Hypodermis

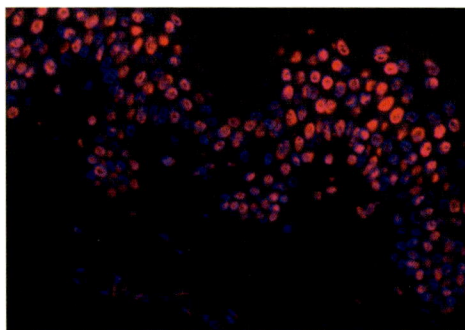

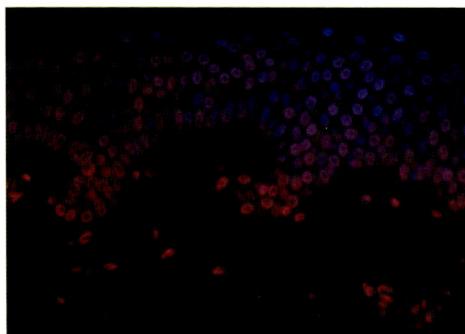

Sunlight causes damage to the skin at different depths (top). Fluorescence microscopy shows damage to DNA caused by Ultraviolet B (middle) and also by the deeper penetrating Ultraviolet A, which was unexpected (bottom)

Climate change and the sun

St John's works closely with Professor Anthony Young, head of photobiology at Kings College, London, who has recently completed a three year, 3.5 million euro project studying the impact of climate change on exposure to ultraviolet radiation.

The project brought together photobiologists, dermatologists, immunologists, epidemiologists and climatologists from six European countries and involved measuring personal exposure to UV by individuals wearing dosimeters. The researchers are analysing the findings in relation to meteorological, environmental and behavioural factors and their impact on health.

Research led by Professor Young, published in 2011, revealed that UVA caused similar damage to the DNA in skin cells as UVB and could put individuals at risk of cancer. Previously UVB was thought to be the cause of skin cancer.

The research showed that UVA, previously thought to cause wrinkles and premature ageing but not cancer, could be more damaging than UVB because the rays penetrated to deeper layers of the skin.

The finding has implications for sun protection because many sunscreens do not contain enough UVA protection. Most people do not put on nearly enough lotion, he said.

The nucleotide excision repair pathway

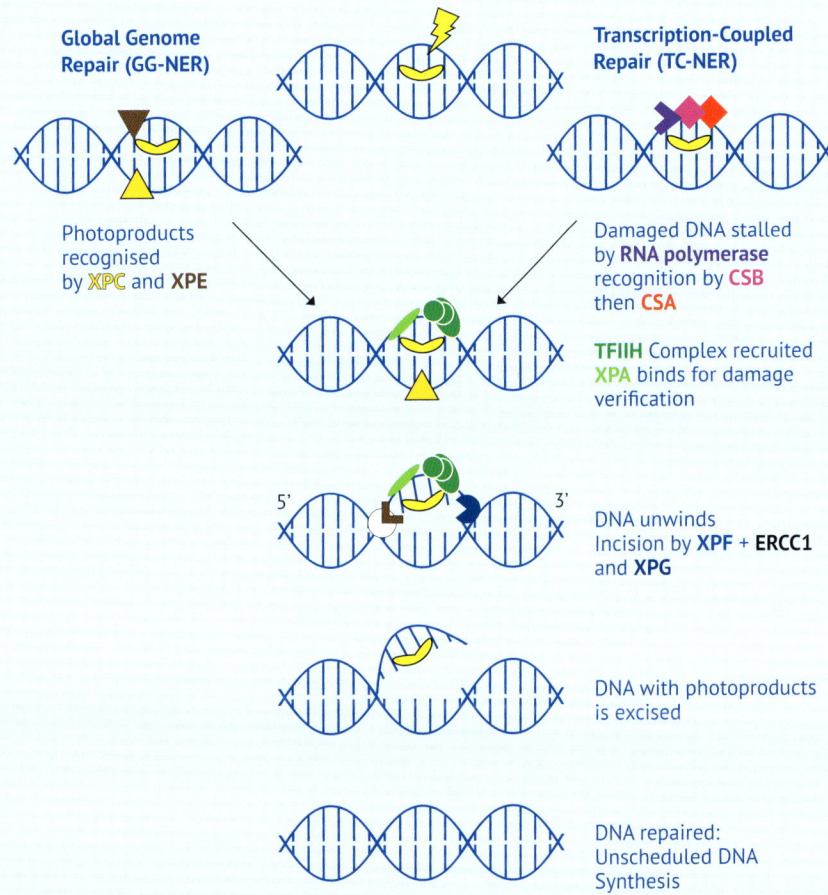

Global Genome Repair (GG-NER)

Transcription-Coupled Repair (TC-NER)

Photoproducts recognised by XPC and **XPE**

Damaged DNA stalled by **RNA polymerase** recognition by CSB then **CSA**

TFIIH Complex recruited XPA binds for damage verification

5'

3'

DNA unwinds Incision by **XPF** + **ERCC1** and **XPG**

DNA with photoproducts is excised

DNA repaired: Unscheduled DNA Synthesis

The Nucleotide Excision Repair Pathway: a key mechanism that removes DNA damaged by ultraviolet light. When it fails owing to in-born genetic errors, severe human disease such as Xeroderma Pigmentosum results

Photoproducts

RNA polymerase

Cockayne Syndrome Protein A (**CSA**)

Cockayne Syndrome Protein A (**CSB**)

XPE

XPC

XPA

TFIIH (XPB+XPD+8 other components)

XPF+**ERCC1**

XPG

THE SCALPEL AND THE BEAM OF LIGHT

Mohs surgery

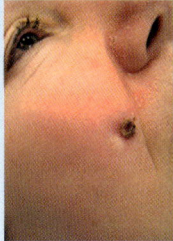
Kathleen before surgery

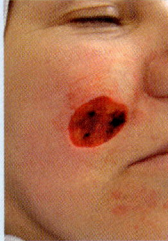
Kathleen after surgery

Kathleen today

CASE STUDY - **KATHLEEN MORREY**

It was only a small lump on her cheek but it was fortunate that Kathleen Morrey, 62, got it checked. She was referred to a consultant in Liverpool, where she lives, and was diagnosed with a high-risk basal cell carcinoma, the commonest kind of skin cancer.

That was bad news but what followed was worse. The former civil servant was warned the surgery necessary to remove the tumour, which was close to her upper lip, was likely to be disfiguring.

"I was so worried about how it would change my face. I remember them telling me they would not be able to do a pretty job. I was devastated," she said.

It was at that point her husband Jim read about the specialist treatment available at St John's Institute for Dermatology in London. It seemed to offer a glimmer of hope. She was referred for Mohs Micrographic Surgery - a technique in which the skin is removed layer by layer in slices as thin as 1mm. The surgeon examines each layer under the microscope for the presence of cancer cells before removing the next, ensuring that all cancerous tissue is excised whilst the surrounding healthy tissue is left intact.

Kathleen had her operation under local anaesthetic, was given the all clear the same day and the area was repaired without a skin graft.

Conventional surgery would have left her with a bigger wound, as it would have required a 4-6mm margin around the lesion rather than the narrow margin possible with Mohs.

The edges of her tumour were also difficult to see so the conventional approach would have carried a higher risk of leaving cancerous cells behind.

Kathleen's operation was carried out in 2008. In May 2013, she passed the five year mark without a recurrence. She remains well and the cancer is now unlikely to return.

"If my husband had not seen that article about St John's I would have had no choice but to go through with the other treatment. I am so grateful for the love and support I received throughout my skin cancer ordeal," she said.

Raj Mallipeddi, the Mohs surgeon at St John's who led the procedure, said: "Kathleen's tumour was the ideal type to be removed by Mohs surgery. Seeing her reach the five year marker shows how excellent the outcome has been for her".

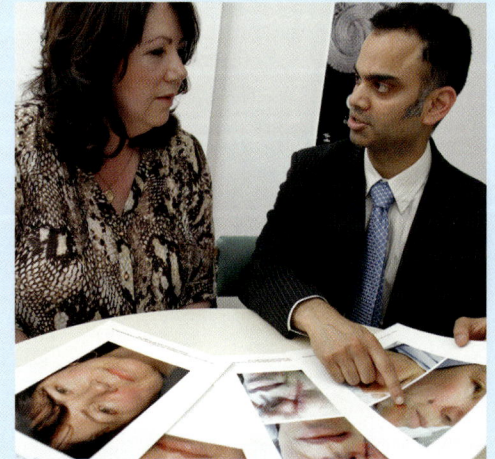
Kathleen with Dr Raj Mallipeddi: conventional surgery would have left her with a bigger scar

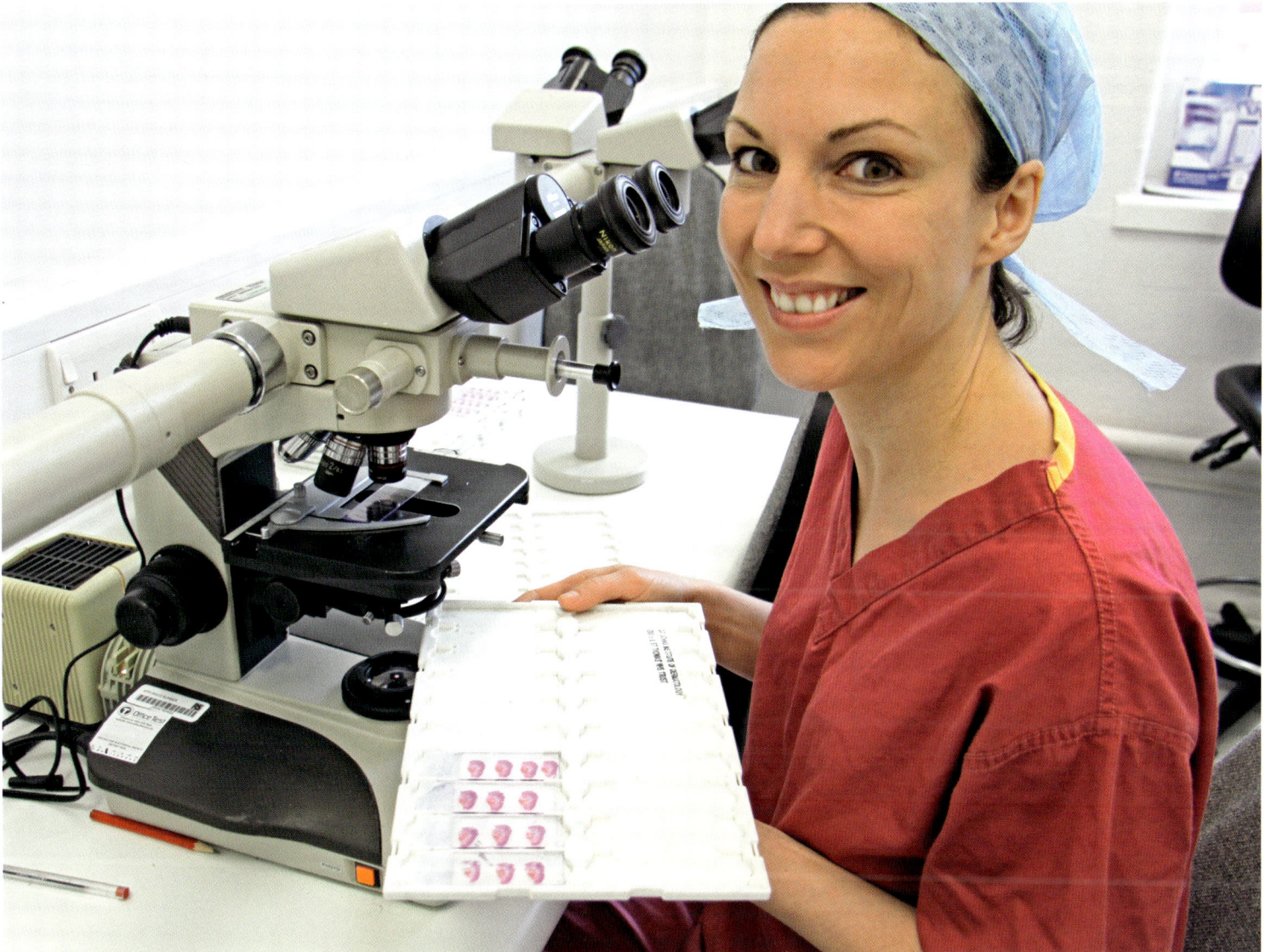

Emma Craythorne: the types of patients seen at St John's have changed. Forty years ago skin rashes accounted for nine out of ten. Today half are investigated for suspected skin cancer

Mohs surgery

The growing burden of skin cancer

The types of patients treated by dermatologists at St John's have changed dramatically over the decades. Forty years ago, skin rashes accounted for nine out of ten. Today, half of all referrals are for suspected skin cancers. More than 12,500 patients were treated for the disease at St John's last year.

The population is growing older and there have been sharp increases in skin cancers at all ages. In addition, modern techniques mean that patients who would once have been admitted to hospital and treated under general anaesthetic can now be treated as out-patients.

The development of Mohs surgery is an example of this. It owes its name to **Frederic Mohs**, a general surgeon, who pioneered the approach in the US in 1938 while still a medical student at the University of Wisconsin-Madison.

He used a paste containing zinc chloride and bloodroot to stain the area of the lesion, and then divided it into segments, like a pizza. Instead of cutting vertically into the tumour – the conventional approach – he cut horizontally, removing the skin layer by layer and examining it for signs of cancer cells under the microscope.

Patients had to wait 24 or 48 hours for each tissue section to be 'proved' before it could be examined, requiring repeat visits. Today, the tissue is frozen using a cryostat and can be examined within an hour so the treatment can be completed the same day.

Skin cancers often grow to uneven depths so patients end up with more horizontal slices removed from the pizza in some areas than others.

Frederic Mohs   Christopher Zachary

But the advantage is that only cancerous tissue is taken by the Mohs surgeon – who also acts as his or her own pathologist.

Raj Mallipeddi, consultant dermatological surgeon, said: "As you remove the layers of skin , if you find you still have cancerous tissue you can take more very accurately just from that position. Around high risk areas such as the eyes, nose, ears and mouth every millimetre counts in terms of tissue conservation and at these precious sites it is essential to remove all of the cancerous cells. "

"That's the beauty of Mohs - how far you go is driven entirely by the cancer. Then you can reconstruct the defect safe in the knowledge that you have removed all of the cancer."

How Mohs surgery spread

Frederic Mohs spent his life promoting the technique he described, teaching it to doctors from all over the world. Nevertheless it was several decades before a modified procedure was accepted by the mainstream. This was introduced to St John's in the 1980s by **Christopher Zachary** (pictured above), following a fellowship in the US and with the help of the then Dean, Professor Malcolm Greaves.

Sean Whittaker, consultant dermatologist, said: "I remember his discussions with Malcolm Greaves [then head of the department] who was a physician and complained that it sounded unusually complicated. Chris was a larger than life character and he gave a wonderful lecture on the subject. From then on, Malcolm was hooked."

Zachary's immediate successors were Neil Walker, who maintained the Mohs service and introduced the laser service and Andrew Markey who was responsible for the design of the current unit. The clinical service and academic profile were further developed over subsequent years by Richard Barlow, Habib Kurwa and most recently Raj Mallipeddi, the incumbent lead clinician. It is now the largest Mohs service in the UK performing over 1000 operations per year. The unit currently has four Mohs surgeons **Raj Mallipeddi**, **Richard Barlow**, **Emma Craythorne** and **Nisith Sheth**. The unit is responsible for training the next generation of Mohs surgeons and has two 1-year fellowship trainees at any time.

As well as *basal cell carcinomas*, the Mohs technique is also suitable for *squamous cell carcinomas*, *lentigo maligna* and rarer cancers such as *dermatofibrosarcoma protruberans*.

The next stage in the development of Mohs surgery is being pioneered at St Johns to speed up the examination and diagnosis of the removed skin slices. The Institute has acquired several confocal scanning microscopes, the first of their kind in the country.

The device can "see" into the skin, acquiring images from different depths. This enables it to

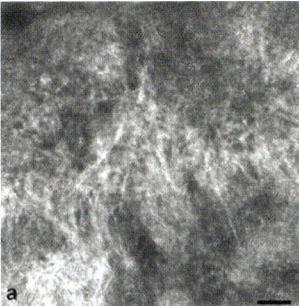

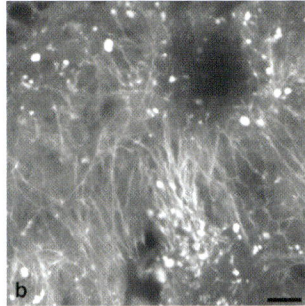

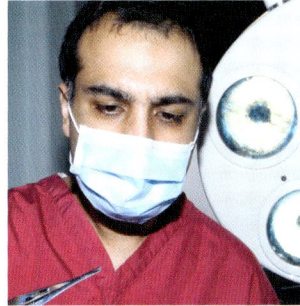

a b
c d
Seeing into the skin at different depths

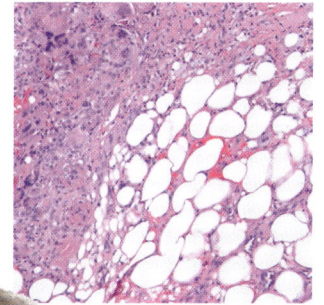

Nisith Sheth

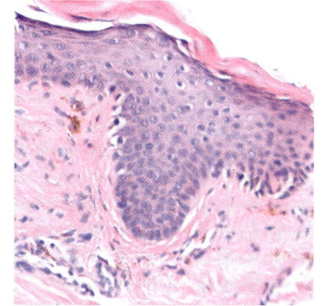

Lentigo maligna

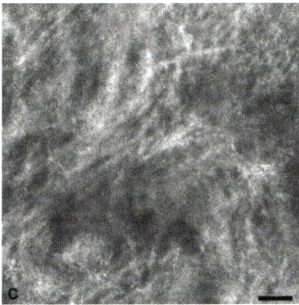

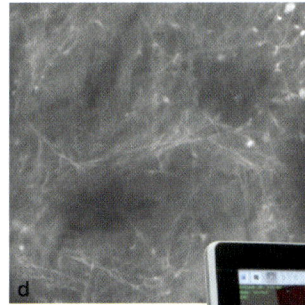

Dermatofibrosarcoma Protuberans

scan removed tissue for signs of cancer in three minutes so that patients do not have to leave the theatre while the surgeon examines the specimens and the operation can be completed without interruption.

Nisith Sheth, consultant dermatological surgeon, said: "It is very early days and we are still in the research stage. But it is very exciting. We are the only Trust to have this microscope."

St John's is the only hospital in the country to have confocal scanning microscopes which can see into the skin at different depths, speeding diagnosis

Mohs Surgery: THE PROCESS

Step 1: Skin cancers can form roots which extend beyond the visible portion of the tumour. If these microscopic roots are left behind, the skin cancer will recur. What is seen visually from the surface of the skin does not always represent what is present microscopically, like a "tip of the iceberg."

TOP VIEW

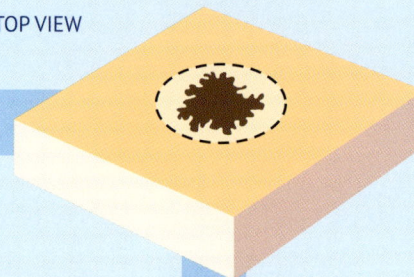

SIDE VIEW

SIDE VIEW   TOP VIEW   BOTTOM VIEW

ORIENTATION NICK

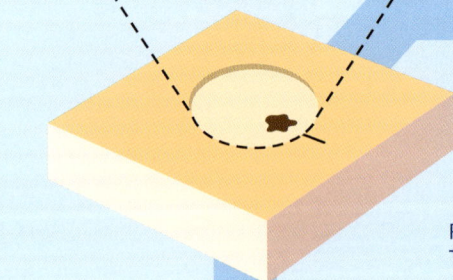

Step 2: The visible portion of the cancer is first removed in a thin "pancake-like" layer. A small nick is placed in the specimen and the wound bed for orientation. A map of the surgical site is then drawn.

RESIDUAL TUMOUR

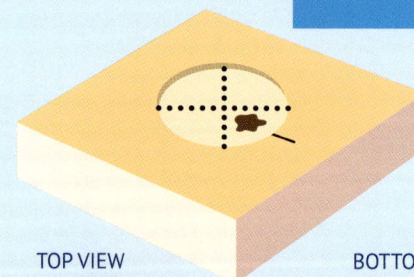

Step 3: The removed layer of skin is taken to the Mohs laboratory where it is colour coded and sectioned for processing. The tissue sections are then stained and made into slides for the surgeon to review.

TOP VIEW

BOTTOM VIEW

Step 4: Each of the 4 sections are microscopically examined for evidence of remaining cancer. All of the edges and undersurface are analysed to ensure complete tumour removal. Sections 1, 2 and 3 are clear, but section 4 has a small focus of tumour at the base. This area is marked on the Mohs map.

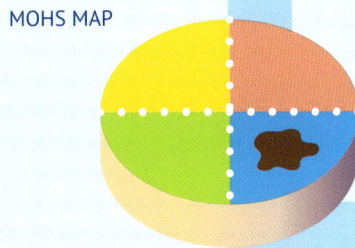

MOHS MAP

HEALTHY TISSUES SAVED FROM EXCISION

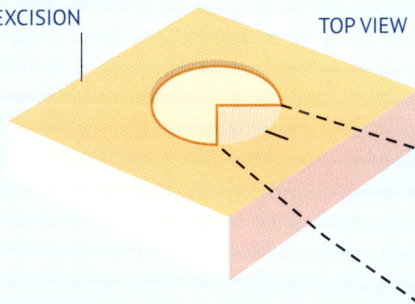

TOP VIEW

TOP VIEW

BOTTOM VIEW

SIDE VIEW

HEALTHY TISSUES SAVED FROM EXCISION

Step 5: The Mohs surgeon returns to the patient to remove another layer of skin. Using the Mohs map, surgery is now limited to precisely where the cancer cells remain. The rest of the surgical site is left alone to conserve the maximum amount of normal tissue. The specimen then returns to the lab for processing and staining again.

Step 6: The tumour in section 4 is not present on the bottom or the peripheral margins. Section 4 is now clear of cancer in the surgical margins, and the removal process is over. The surgical wound will now be evaluated for reconstruction options.

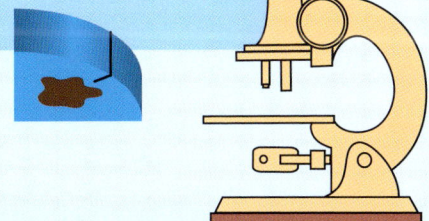

Laser Treatment

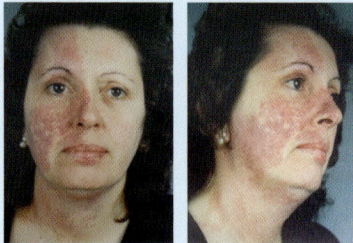

Ann before treatment: "If only they had invented it when I was a child"

CASE STUDY - **ANN LAYTON**

Ann Layton of Felixstowe, Suffolk, was born with a large birthmark covering the right side of her face and extending up into her scalp. Now aged 69, she still recalls the agony of coping with her disfigurement as a child.

"It was very difficult. At boarding school there was nowhere to hide. The pupils were quite sympathetic – the headmaster warned them about bullying – but people would sometimes say: 'Who's bashed you in the face?'"

From the age of four she was taught to use make-up. She has spent much of her life since living under cover. "I wouldn't open the door to people till I had got my make up on. When I was first married my husband didn't know for some weeks about the birthmark. I never allowed him to see me without make up. I was very hung up on it."

As a child she remembers being treated with a "radioactive liquid" that was smeared on her face and left in place. "I was not allowed to wash my face for ten days. But it didn't do much."

Then in 1988 a TV programme was broadcast about a new Argon laser being used to treat skin conditions.

"I was bombarded with calls from friends asking if I had seen it and suggesting I go for treatment. So I did."

For the next decade she went regularly every six months for treatment which turned out to be a punishing regime. The primitive laser could only treat an area the size of a 50 pence piece at a time and it worked by effectively burning the skin.

"It was very painful. A blister came up after each treatment so you couldn't put make up on. I had to wait for days afterwards. I kept going for ten years – it made some improvement but not a lot."

In the late 90s she heard St John's had acquired a new Pulsed Dye laser which offered significant advantages over the old Argon laser. She got herself referred again. This time the treatment worked.

"It was completely different. The whole area was targeted in one go and I had six weeks between treatments. There was a bruising effect but no pain. I improved quite a lot".

Two years ago she was seen for review and has had 9 more treatments at St John's provided by consultant Emma Craythorne. "There was no pain. It was like someone pinging an elastic band against your skin. Dr Craythorne said: 'We are going to make the skin perfect' and to be quite honest that is what they have achieved."

"If only they had invented this when I was a little child. It would have saved all the hassle."

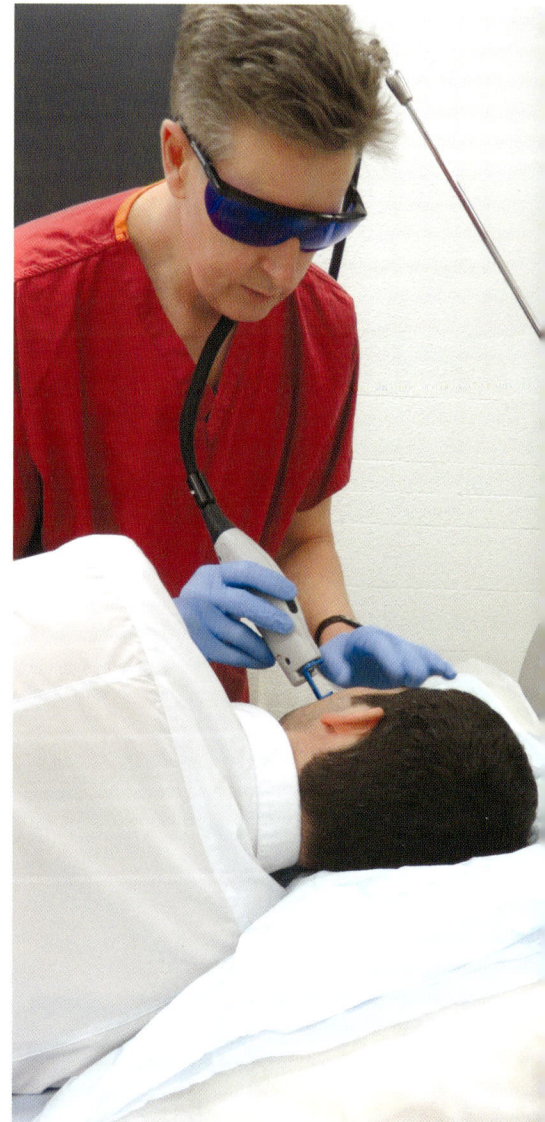

Richard Barlow with the Pulsed Dye Laser: used to lighten port wine stains and similar lesions

Treatment with a beam of light

Lasers, which emit a beam of high-intensity light, have come a long way from their beginnings 40 years ago. The first Argon lasers of the type used to treat Ann Layton had a serious side effect. They often caused unsightly scars to form. Today's devices are more sophisticated and selective, emitting beams of specific wavelengths which can be targeted more accurately to treat different conditions.

St John's is one of the largest laser units in London and a referral centre for the whole UK. It has six types of laser – each with a specific target. The wide range of wavelengths available allows very close matching to the absorption characteristics of certain tissues, such as melanin or haemoglobin, and the narrow bandwidth that can be obtained minimises damage to the surrounding tissue.

The Institute offers treatment for birth marks such as port wine stains, *haemangiomas* (a swelling formed by an abnormal collection of blood vessels), pigment disorders causing brown on the skin, *keloids* (bumpy scars) and unwanted hair (of a severer kind than that treated in beauty clinics).

Much of the treatment is carried out by highly skilled clinical nurse specialists who have been trained in laser techniques and who run the laser clinics – an example of how nurses are increasingly taking on roles that were once restricted to doctors.

The Q-switched lasers are used to treat pigmentary lesions such as freckles, brown patches on the skin, and *Naevis of Ota*, a condition which manifests as dark patches on the face and around the eyes. It is also used to remove tattoos.

The laser beam's wavelength is set to target brown colour so it is absorbed by cells containing melanin in the skin which are selectively destroyed, leaving the rest of the skin unaffected.

The Q switching technique allows the production of a pulsed beam of light of higher power than would be possible with a continuous beam, which can penetrate the skin to greater depths without damaging healthy tissue. In the case of tattoo removal it shatters the tattoo pigment into tiny particles which can then be cleared by the body's lymphatic system. Full removal can take between six and twenty treatments depending on the amount and colour of the ink, with a month between treatments.

The Pulsed Dye Laser is used to lighten port wine stains and similar vascular lesions by targeting the redness of the blood vessels just below the skin. The laser causes the blood vessels in the lesion to heat up which destroys them, leaving a bruise which fades over a few weeks. The laser produces significant lightening of the lesions without affecting the skin's texture or causing scarring and is

safe enough to be given to young infants.

The V-beam laser is a new, refined version of the pulsed dye laser which has a greater variety of settings to deliver more energy in a more targeted fashion. It is the gold standard pulsed dye laser treatment for a wide variety of vascular lesions.

Richard Barlow said: "There was a much higher risk of scarring with laser treatment in the past. Now lasers are more precise with targeted treatment so that normal tissue around the lesion is less affected. The energy is delivered more where is it needed, dramatically improving safety."

Intense pulsed light, often abbreviated to IPL, is used for hair removal and to treat vascular lesions. It is not a true laser because the pulses are distributed over a range of wavelengths. The broad spectrum light penetrates the skin and is absorbed by the melanin concentrated in the hair roots which heat up and are destroyed.

The Alexandrite laser is a more sophisticated hair removal device which is better targeted on the brown colour of the melanin at the base of the hair follicle. The stronger the treatment the greater the

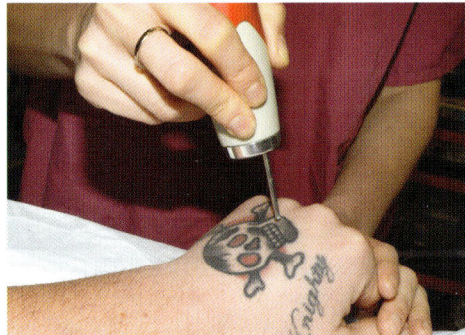

The Q-switched laser: to treat freckles and remove tattoos

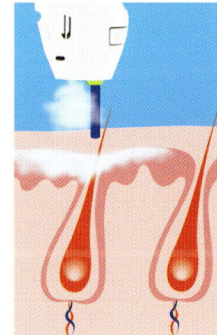

The Pulsed Dye Laser:
targets the blood vessels

likelihood of side effects such as redness, swelling and tenderness but these subside after a few days. Added cooling systems with each laser make treatment quicker than in the past and reduce side effects, so patients can return to work and normal activities sooner.

The **CO2 laser** targets water in the tissues and has an ablative (burning) effect. It is used to treat big keloid scars which would otherwise have to be cut out with a scalpel. The laser does the same job in a bloodless way, as the beam cauterises as it cuts. It is also used for skin resurfacing – essentially burning the skin to promote collagen formation – as a treatment for wrinkles, sun damage and warts.

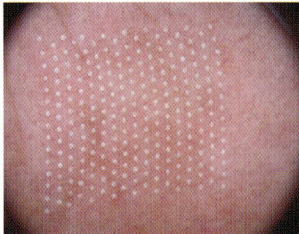

The CO2 laser (above and right) : treats wrinkles, sun damage and warts as well as big keloid scars. It targets the water in the tissues and has a burning effect.

Skin imaging

Before a patient with skin cancer can be treated the diagnosis must be confirmed. This is normally carried out by taking a biopsy – surgically removing a sample of skin which is then examined under the microscope for signs of cancer. The process is painful, potentially scarring and causes delays.

Now St John's has an alternative
The **in-vivo reflectance confocal microscope** is described as opening a "window into the skin".

The device allows the surgeon to examine a mole or other skin lesion directly, by placing the microscope onto it, which can then "see" through the epidermis down into the layers below.

The microscope scans down through the lesion and can reveal individual cells down to the upper reticular dermis. This enables the surgeon to painlessly examine the living tissue layers avoiding the need for biopsies.

Emma Craythorne said: "Devices such as this can improve our pick up rate of malignant lesions . We need to minimise the false alarms while ensuring no cancers are missed. The use of these skin imaging techniques is going to make that more likely."

Patients with *lentigo maligna*, a precursor of melanoma are among the early beneficiaries of the technology. *Lentigo maligna* forms a flat lesion usually on the head and neck that may be particularly large.

The Vivascope allows the entire large lesion of *lentigo maligna* to be visualised and the borders accurately delineated . The technology does what all innovative technology should – it enables surgeons to do more with less.

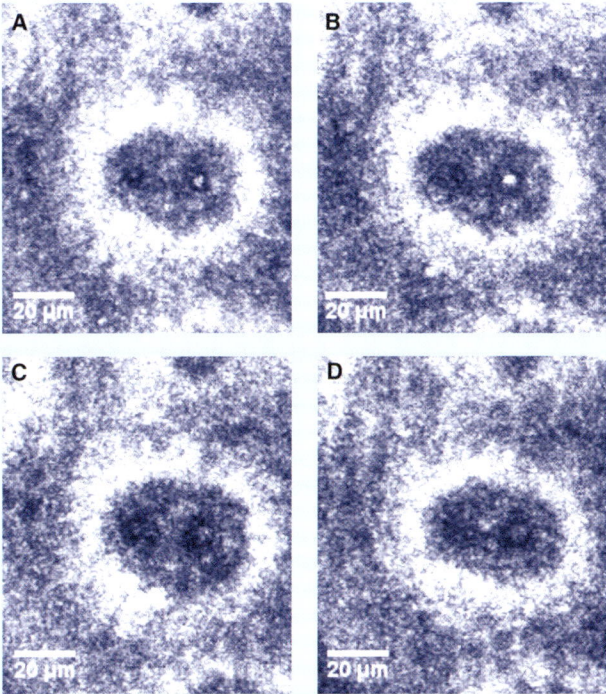

The in-vivo reflectance confocal microscope opens a "window into the skin." The surgeon can examine a mole directly and see through the epidermis into the layers below, removing the need for painful and invasive biopsies.

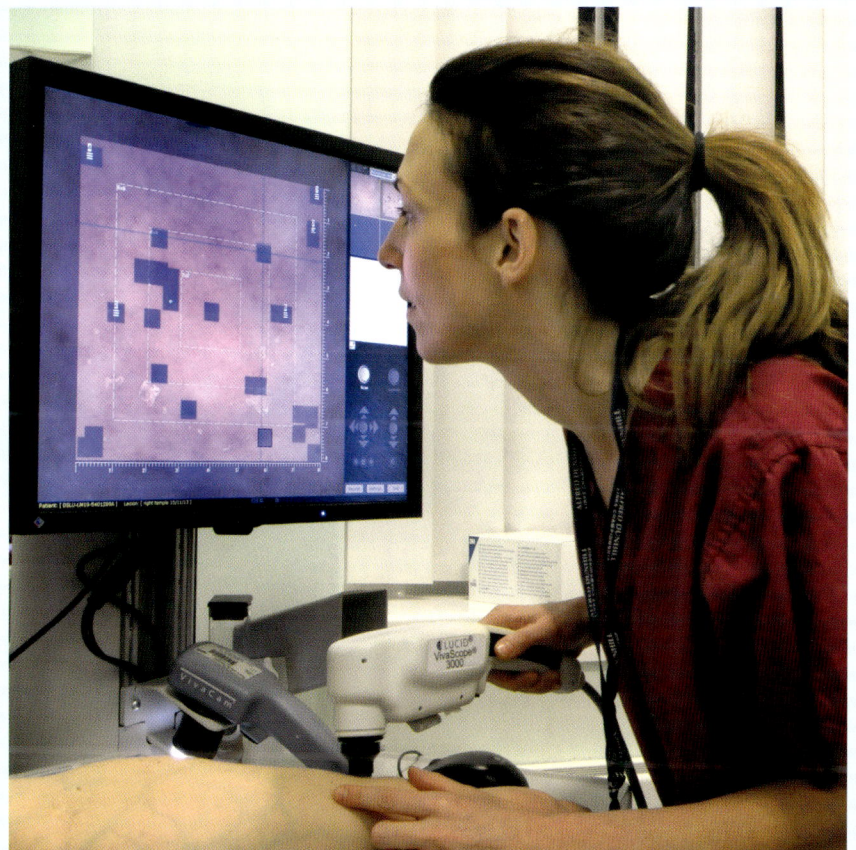

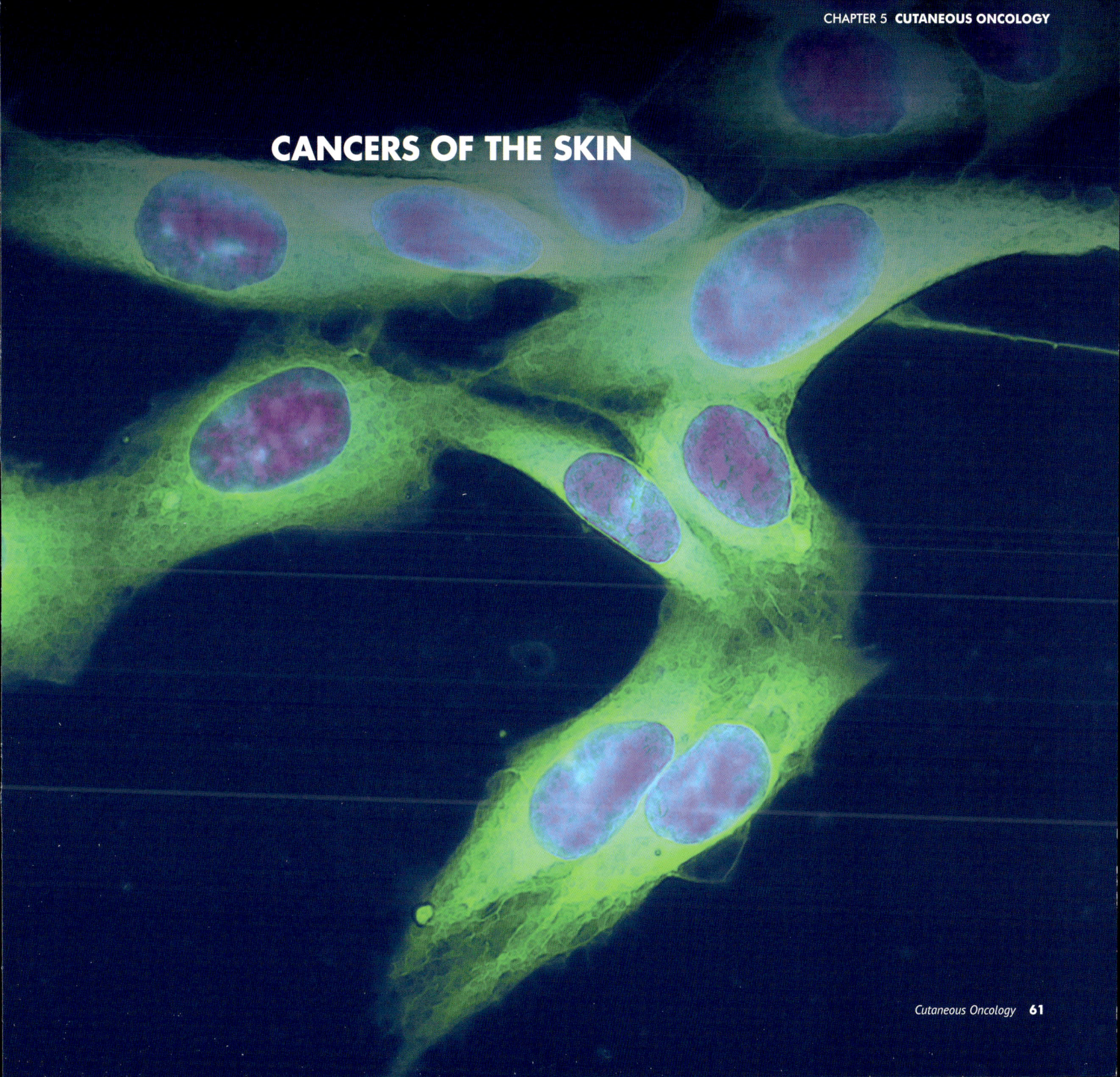

CANCERS OF THE SKIN

Melanoma

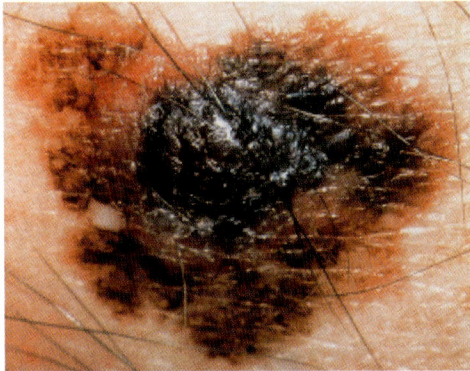

Melanoma – the fastest rising cancer in the UK

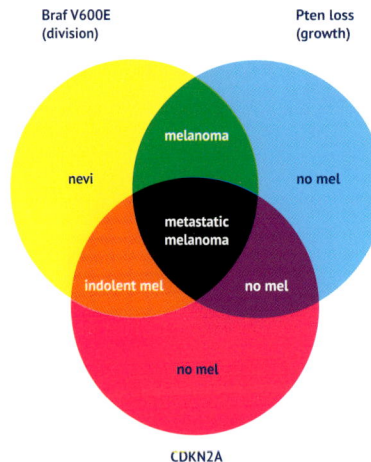

Braf V600E (division) Pten loss (growth)

melanoma

nevi no mel

metastatic melanoma

indolent mel no mel

no mel

CDKN2A

Three different mutations determine, in combination, whether melanoma is slow growing or capable of rapid spread

Melanoma has been the fastest rising cancer in the UK over the past 25 years, with more than 12,000 cases a year and 2,000 deaths. Death rates are 7 per cent higher in men although the incidence of the cancer is the same in both sexes.

Until recently surgery to remove the lesions was the only treatment. But in June 2011, scientists unveiled what has been described as the biggest breakthrough in the treatment of melanoma in 30 years – a twice a day pill that halved the death rate among patients with advanced disease.

Melanoma is the deadliest form of skin cancer, killing one in five of those affected. A typical victim is the pale-skinned office worker who spends two weeks broiling on a Mediterranean beach until their skin is red and blistered.

Men tend to delay going to the doctor and may be more biologically susceptible which could explain their higher death rate. Covering up in the midday sun and using high-factor sun cream is the best defence against the cancer.

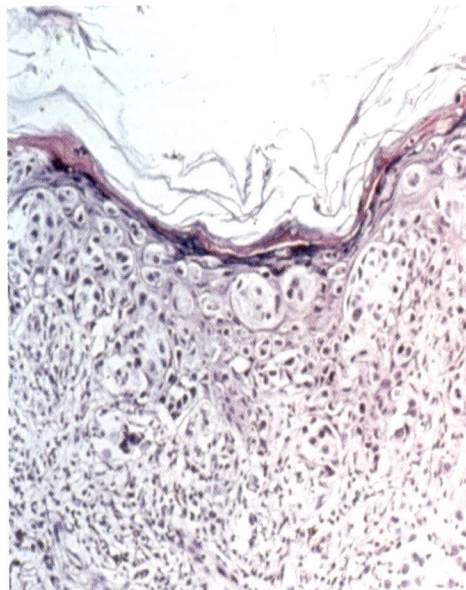

There are 12,000 cases of melanoma and 2,000 deaths a year

The typical victim of melanoma is a pale-skinned office worker who spends two weeks a year broiling on a Mediterranean beach till their skin is red and blistered.

New Drugs

The results of the international trial of the twice a day pill in which St John's was a key partner, showed the drug, vemurafenib, boosted survival rates at six months from 64 per cent to 84 per cent. The improvement was so dramatic that half way through the trial the patients randomly assigned to standard chemotherapy were offered the chance to switch to vemurafenib.

The drug is the first "personalised" treatment for melanoma, designed to target cases of the disease carrying the faulty gene, called a BRAF mutation, which account for about half of all cases. As such, it marks a milestone in the transformation of cancer medicines from blunderbuss treatments for everybody to designer drugs tailored to individual cases.

The findings were published in the New England Journal of Medicine and vemurafenib, marketed as Zelboraf by the multinational pharmaceutical company Roche, was licensed in Europe in 2013.

The development demonstrates the dividends

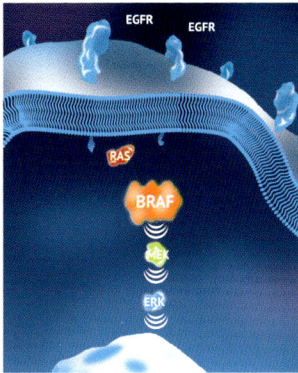

Melanoma is driven by BRAF and NRAS gene mutations in the cell

a Patient 1

Pre-treatment   **2 weeks vemurafenib**

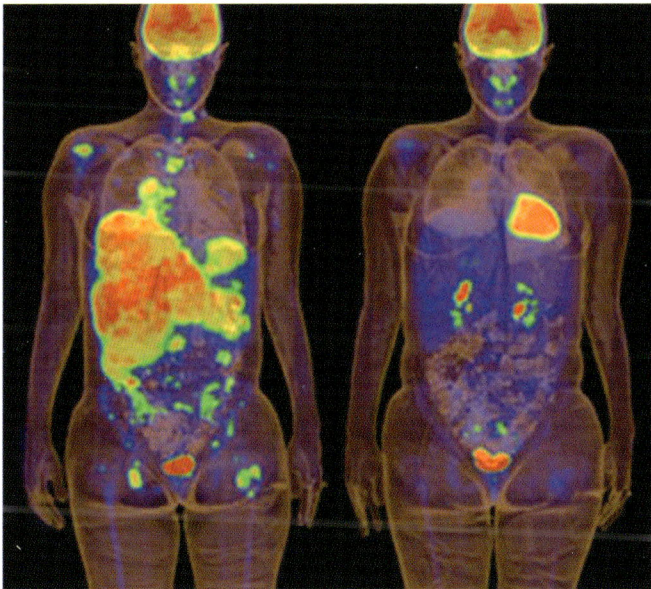

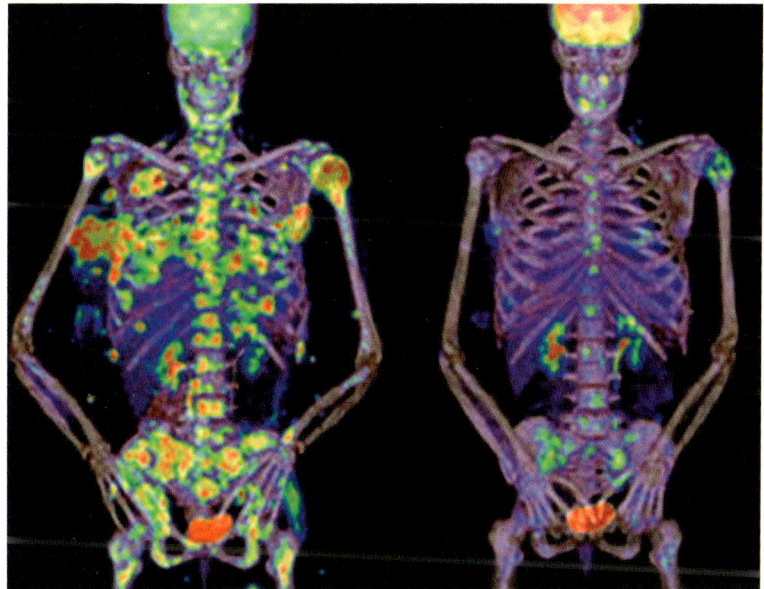

b Patient 2

Pre-treatment   **2 weeks vemurafenib**

These scans show how the drug, vemurafenib, a BRAF inhibitor, reversed the disease in two patients. It has been described as the biggest breakthrough in the treatment of melanoma in 30 years.

that the collaborative spirit fostered by St Johns – across specialties and across the world - can bring.

The melanoma service was started at the Institute in the 1990s by **Neil Smith**, a dermatologist and skin pathologist who happened also to be an accomplished cartoonist. It combined plastic surgery and oncology with dermatology to create an early example of the multidisciplinary service that would become standard throughout the NHS over a decade later.

An early challenge was to understand why surgery to remove the lesions successfully halted the disease in some patients while in others it did not. In the 1970s, surgeons made enormous excisions, leaving unsightly scars, in their effort to rid the body of cancer. But the approach failed and today a border of just 1-2cm of healthy tissue around the lesion is removed.

Professor Sean Whittaker, head of the department, said: "The problem was for those patients who progressed we had no treatment. So the challenge was: could we identify who would progress and do something to help them?"

Cath Morgan

Sukran Sagham

Alison Baker

Ian Gosling

The Clinical Nurse Specialist (CNS) Team in our skin cancer department.

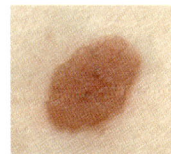
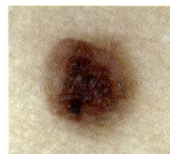
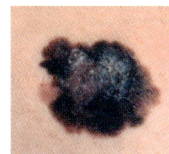

Moles (left to right)
Benign
Dysplastic
Melanoma

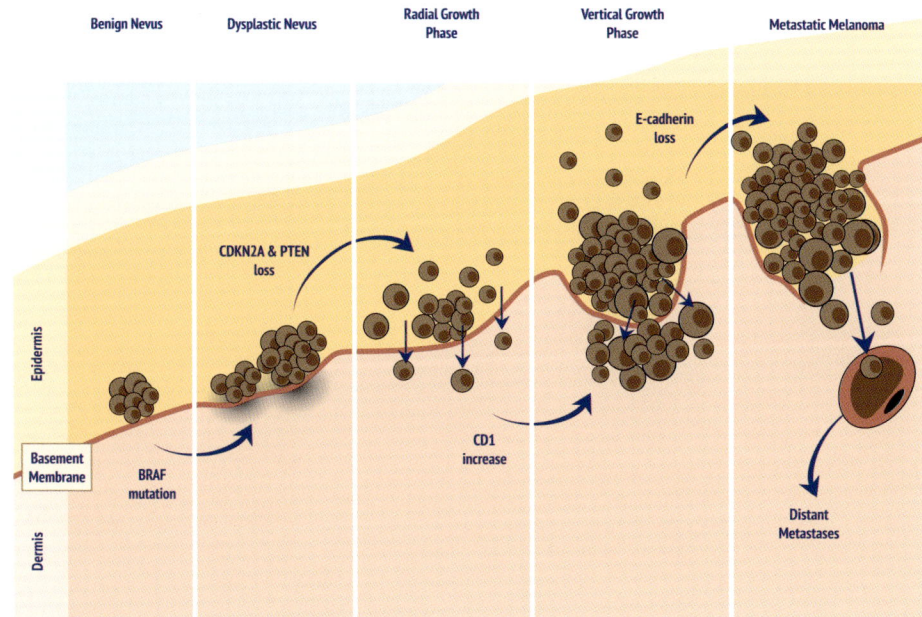

Development of melanoma showing how the disease breaks through the skin's basement membrane and spreads to other organs and distant parts of the body

(From left to right) Edward Wilson-Jones, who developed dermatopathology at St John's, Peter Samman, founder of the lymphoma service, Neil Smith, who started the melanoma service and Margaret Spittle, the pioneer of radiotherapy for skin lymphomas in the UK

A new diagnostic technique

St John's answer was to develop sentinel node biopsy, a technique now widely practised for determining how far melanoma has spread. Surgery is carried out in two stages, ten days apart, with the second operation designed to "sweep up" after the precise extent of the cancerous tissue has been confirmed in the laboratory after the first operation.

Before the second op goes ahead, surgeons inject blue dye with a radioactive tracer at four points around the scar. The tracer is taken up by the lymph glands and its location can be detected with a geiger counter. Surgeons open an incision at that point to expose the pea-sized lymph gland coloured blue with the dye which is removed and checked to see if there is early spread of the cancer. If it is affected, all other lymph glands in the area are removed – a bigger operation with a higher risk of complications.

"Sentinel node biopsy is the most sensitive mechanism we have for predicting the spread of melanoma. If it is negative, the risk is low. If it is positive, the risk goes up substantially. The problem is that the therapeutic implications are limited," said Professor Whittaker.

Surgeons still do not know whether, where the technique indicates spread, removing all the glands is effective. A trial is currently underway but experts are pessimistic about the outcome. "It looks as if further surgery adds no further benefit, but we await the results," said Professor Whittaker.

Critics have argued that if there is no therapeutic potential there is no point in carrying out the test. But Professor Whittaker disagrees.

"Now we have new treatments for melanoma becoming available, accurate prognostic information is very important. We need to select the treatments most likely to benefit the patients."

The latest development in sentinel node biopsy does away with the biopsy and replaces it with a sophisticated scanning technique called Spect CT Scanning. This involves taking two different types of scans and merging the images to provide more precise information about the location of affected lymph nodes.

The technique depends on a marker to identify tumour cells and is still under development. It is important because a patient with a melanoma on their back could find the cancer has spread to any one, or all, of six sites – two either side of the neck, under the arms or in the groin.

"The nightmare scenario is surgery required in all six sites. But this might be reduced to two with Spect CT scanning because it can look in a more sophisticated manner," said Professor Whittaker.

Lymphoma group: Sean Whittaker, Mary Wain, Stephen Morris, Fiona Child, Danuta Orlowska with colleagues.

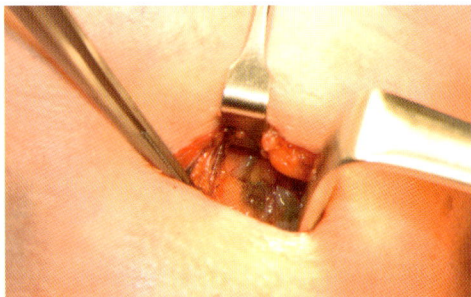
Lymph node biopsy: removal of pea-sized gland to check for cancer

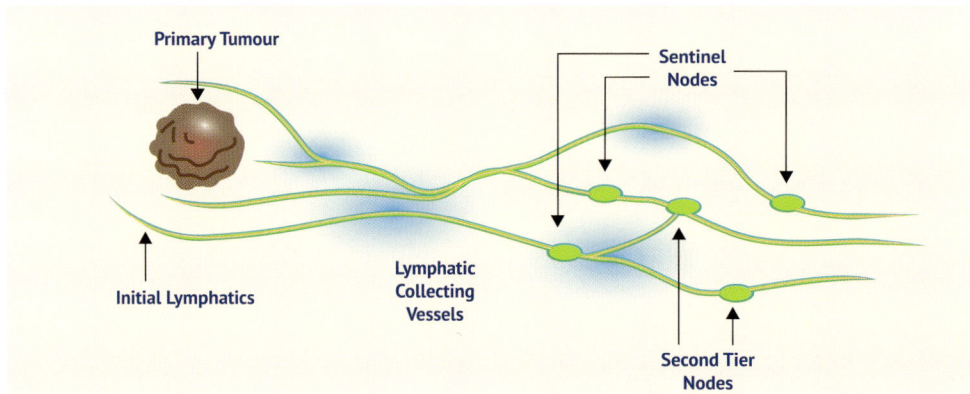
If one lymph gland is affected the others are removed

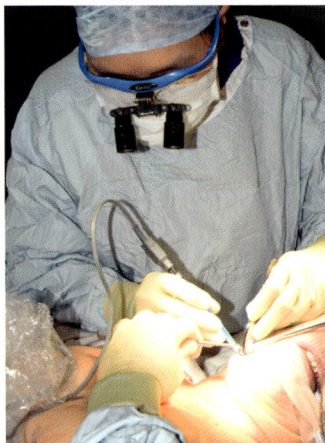
Primary Tumour

Sentinel Nodes

Initial Lymphatics

Lymphatic Collecting Vessels

Second Tier Nodes

Sentinel Nodes Map: in some patients surgery to remove the primary tumour halts the disease. In others, it spreads through the lymphatic system. This map is used to trace its spread

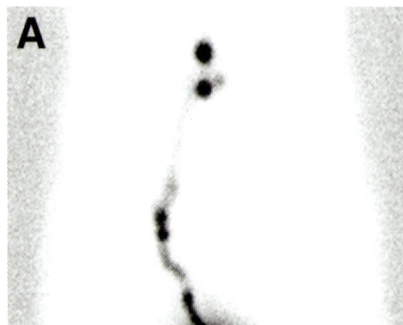
The Spect CT Scanner – a new technique for identifying the spread of cancer to the lymph nodes. It is still under development but could one day lead to more refined surgery

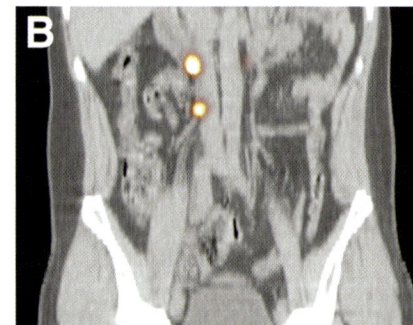
A

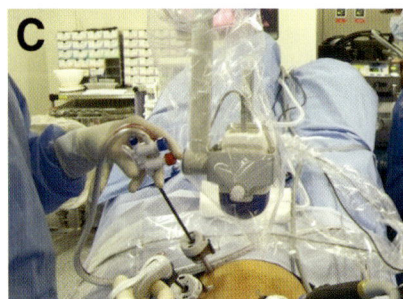
B

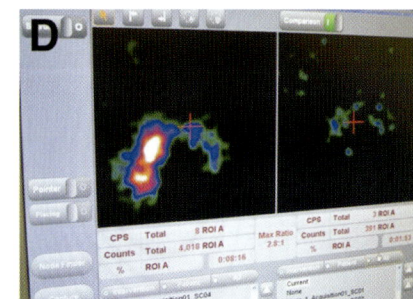
C

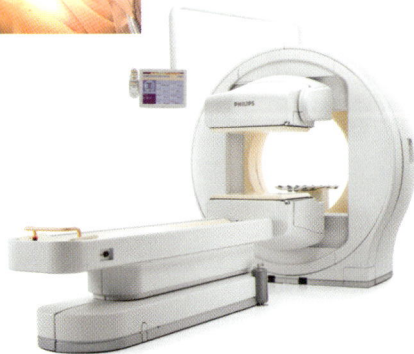
D

Spect CT Scanning involves taking two different types of scans and merging the images to provide more precise information.

Genetic sequencing

Genetic analysis has shown that 60 per cent of melanomas have a BRAF mutation and 20 per cent a NRAS mutation, turning the respective genes into cancer causing oncogenes. By identifying the genetic make-up of a patient's tumour, doctors can select the right targeted treatment for it. Modern sequencing techniques allow this to be done.

In addition to the trial of vemurafenib, a targeted genetic therapy, St John's also participated in studies of immunotherapy – to boost the immune system and enhance its ability to destroy melanoma cells – with the drug ipilimumab, which was

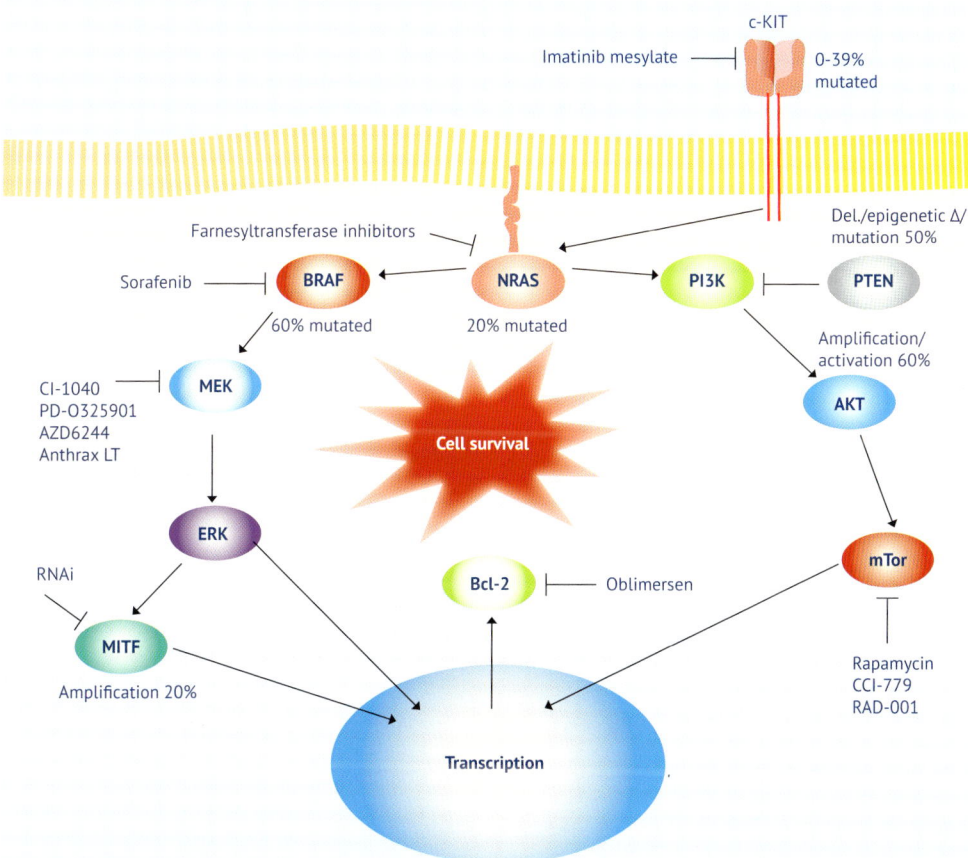

- MHC Class I
- MHC Class II
- T-cell receptor
- Costimulatory molecular
- Melanoma antigen

Targeted immunotherapy has been pioneered at St John's for the worst affected cases and have brought long term benefit

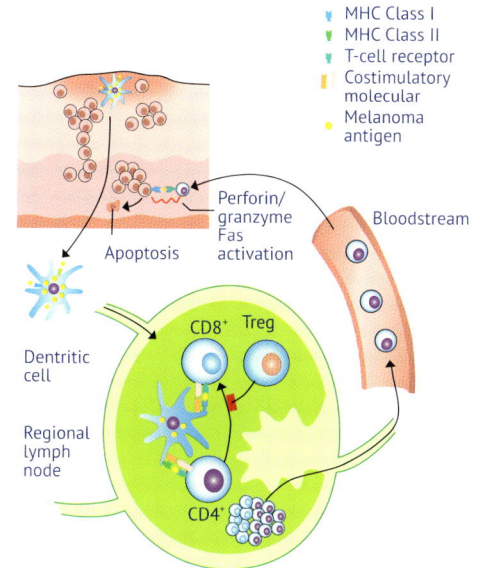

Genetic sequencing has shown that 60 per cent of melanomas have a BRAF mutation and 20 per cent a NRAS mutation. By identifying the genetic make-up, doctors can target the cancer with the right treatment

licensed in Europe in 2011.

In one trial of the drug, made by Bristol Myers Squibb and marketed under the brand name Yervoy, survival at one year was almost doubled from 25 per cent to 46 per cent. However it is expensive at £72,000 for one course of treatment.

Further research is under way into developing antibodies against cancer cells that might be combined with immunotherapy, creating a synergy that enhances the effect of each treatment. The hope is to repeat the success achieved with rituximab in B-cell lymphoma which, when combined with chemotherapy, has proved remarkably effective.

Mole mapping

Melanoma often starts with changes to a mole and people with lots of moles and a family history of the disease are at higher risk, especially if they have clusters of abnormal-looking moles.

As a result researchers are developing a mole mapping service based on an algorithm which could serve as a screening technique.

The idea is that it could be used for high risk patients who would be screened twice a year and may need multiple moles removed. Early diagnosis is essential because if the tumour is less than 1mm thick the cure rate is 90 per cent. If it is over 4mm thick, the cure rate drops to 20 per cent.

But researchers must demonstrate that the algorithm is superior to a visual examination by a specialist.

Existing algorithms are based on criteria derived from visual inspections by experts and are skewed to ensure they are very safe. As a result a patient with many moles who is screened using the algorithm may be advised they need half a dozen removing while a specialist may say only one should be cut out.

For this reason the technique is of little value in screening people at normal risk

Tissue research

Key to any diagnosis of skin cancer, or indeed of any cancer, are the pathologists who check the tissue samples removed at biopsy or in surgery for signs of malignant cells.

St John's has built up a tissue bank of over 15,000

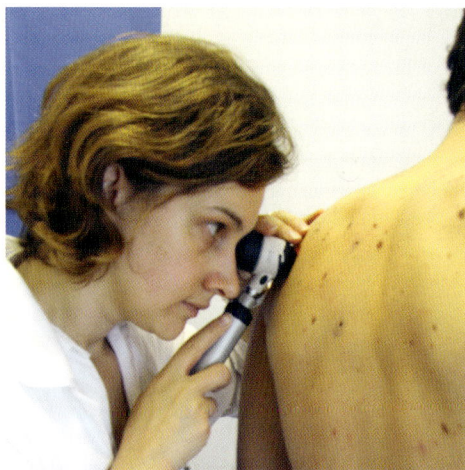

Katie Lacy examining a patient in her melanoma clinic

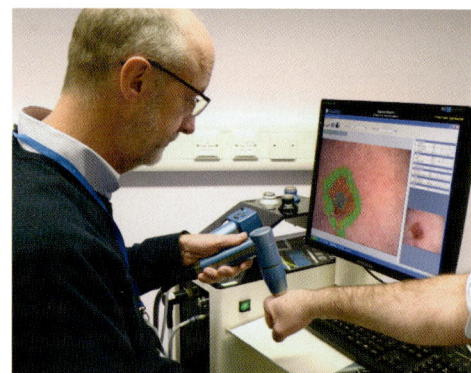

Mole mapping: melanoma often starts with changes to a mole

samples of all types of skin disease, especially melanoma and lymphoma, which has become a national resource.

All the samples, which include blood, lymph and skin, are of unused tissue taken for therapeutic or diagnostic reasons. They are retained for research only with the consent of the patient and are anonymised, categorised and ethically approved.

"It is very important that patients understand this – samples are never taken except as part of diagnosis or treatment. The unused portion may then be retained for research, but only with the consent of the patient," Professor Whittaker said.

Between 3,000 and 4,000 samples come from other hospitals in the UK and overseas and the tissue bank is the largest of its kind in the UK. It was developed in cancer before being extended to cover other areas such as psoriasis.

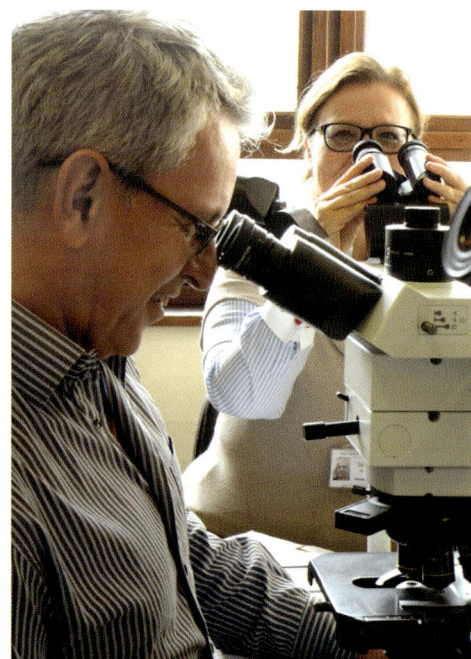

Consultant Dermatopathologists: Eduardo Calonje (head of service) and Catherine Stefanato at the microscope

Non-Melanoma skin cancers

These are extremely common with 100,000 cases a year in the UK. The number has increased by more than a third in the past decade, partly as a result of improved registration but also from increased exposure to the sun and use of sunbeds.

However, over 90 per cent are curable, mostly with surgery to remove the lesion. The majority are *basal cell skin cancers* accounting for three quarters of the total. They impose a huge burden on the NHS.

Some patients have a genetic predisposition to basal cell cancer and develop extensive lesions, some of them large. In such cases surgical removal is difficult because of its mutilating effect.

Research has revealed the mechanism underlying basal cell cancer which is driven by a cluster of gene mutations and led to the development of a drug, vismogedib, which blocks the signal from the mutations and stops the cancer growing.

A topical version of the drug, which is applied directly to the skin, proved ineffective, but an oral version has cleared up lesions in patients with extensive disease. Vismogedib was licensed in Europe and the UK in 2013.

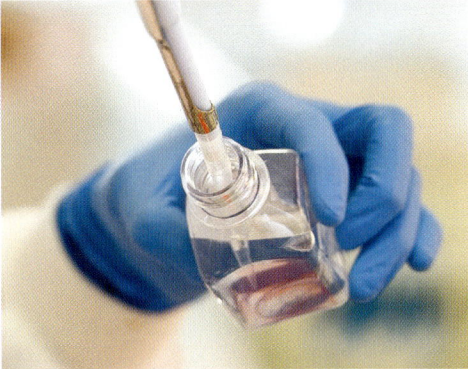

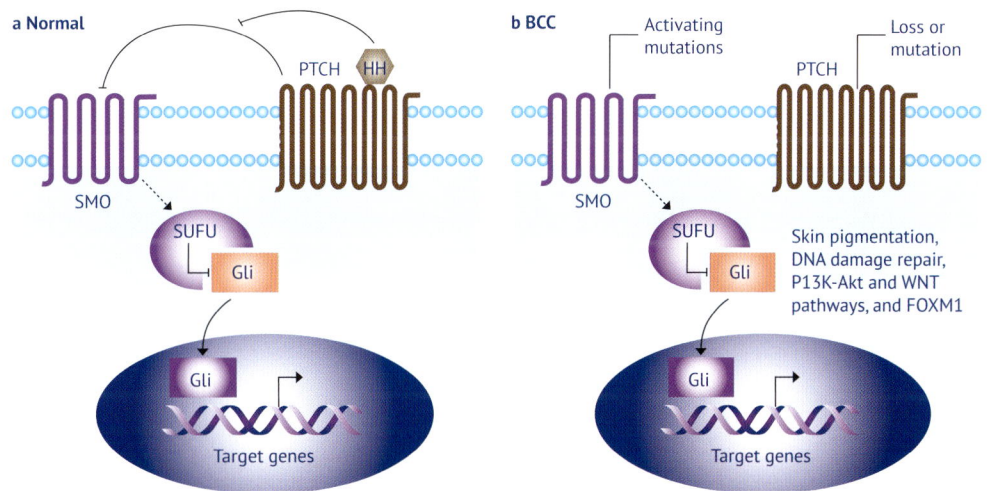

St John's has the largest skin cancer tissue bank in the UK with over 15,000 samples

The samples are studied by dermatopathologists who have been critical to the success of the Cutaneous Oncology department. Advances in molecular pathology over the last 20 years have transformed the outlook for many patients and St John's is now exporting its expertise overseas. The institute has established international programmes for dermatopathology education in Europe, Asia and the Far East.

Hedgehog Signalling Pathway – this is implicated in the development of basal cell carcinoma, the commonest kind of skin cancer, with at least 75,000 cases a year

Cutaneous Lymphona

This is a rare cancer of the lymphocytes (white blood cells) that primarily affects the skin. It is a kind of non-Hodgkin's lymphoma and affects 500-600 people a year in the UK of whom at least a third are treated at St John's.

It typically causes red, scaly skin patches similar to eczema or chronic dermatitis but a third of patients progress to more advanced disease. In severe cases extensive ulceration, itching and infections develop.

In its worst form, *cutaneous lymphoma* may lead to melon-sized tumours, involve the whole skin which becomes red and inflamed from top to toe, the hands swell and split and patients develop a leonine face. The lymph nodes and internal organs may also be affected.

The commonest type of cutaneous lymphoma is *Mycosis Fungoides*. Paul Eddington, star of the 1980s TV sitcom "Yes, minister," was a sufferer.

Professor Whittaker said: "It can be a dreadful, Medieval disease – the worst affected patients have caused health workers to faint. They may have as many as 25 tumours the size of oranges on their skin which can be painful."

The disease is treatable but not curable and has a 35 per cent death rate. It is resistant to chemotherapy but susceptible to radiotherapy which is the mainstay of treatment.

An early pioneer of radiotherapy for the disease was **Margaret Spittle**, who became an iconic female figure in the medical establishment. A Clinical Oncologist (radiotherapist) by training she went to Stanford University in California in the 1970s and returned with a technique of irradiating the whole body known as Total Skin Electron Beam Therapy (TSEB).

Professor Whittaker said: "There was a tradition at St John's of adopting specialists in other disciplines to work with dermatologists. The consultants felt isolated – so they looked for others with whom to work. That was part of how St John's became a multi-specialist discipline."

Electrons penetrate only 1mm into the skin so have a negligible impact on the underlying tissue. But administering TSEB is complex because bodies are curved and lumpy, requiring sophisticated physics.

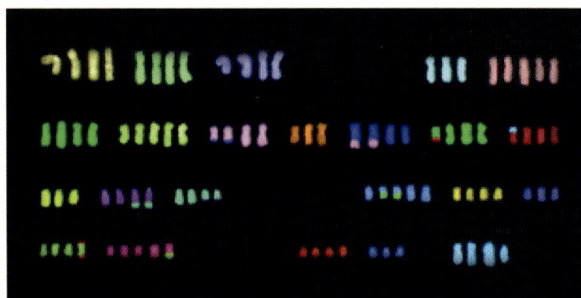

Margaret Spittle

Abnormal chromosomes from a patient with a cutaneous lymphoma, a rare skin cancer affecting 500-600 people in the UK of whom one third are seen at St John's

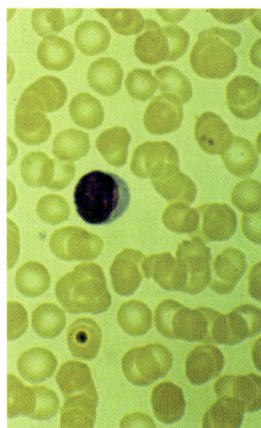

Cutaneous lymphoma cell in blood

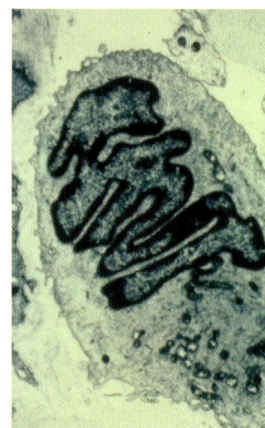

Electron microscopy image of abnormal nucleus

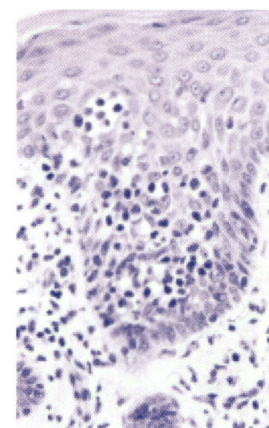

Lymphoma cells in skin

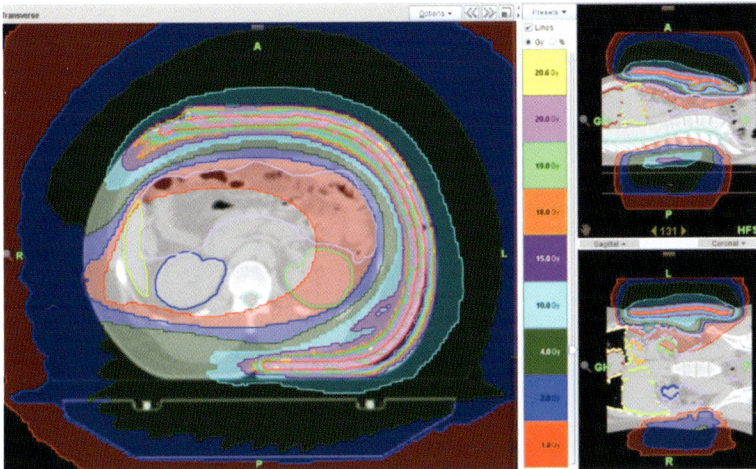

Tomotherapy for mycosis fungoides

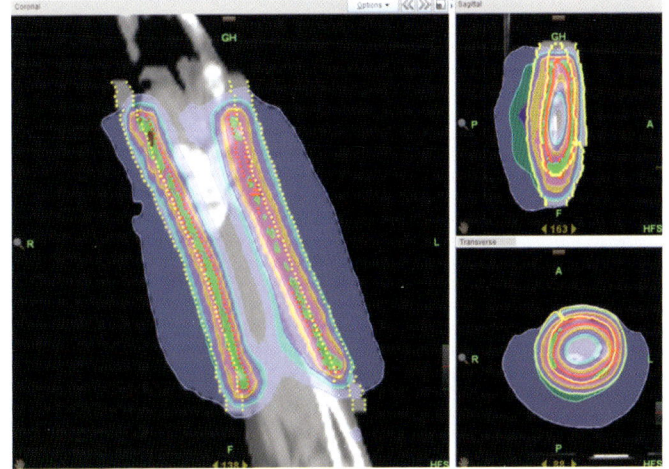

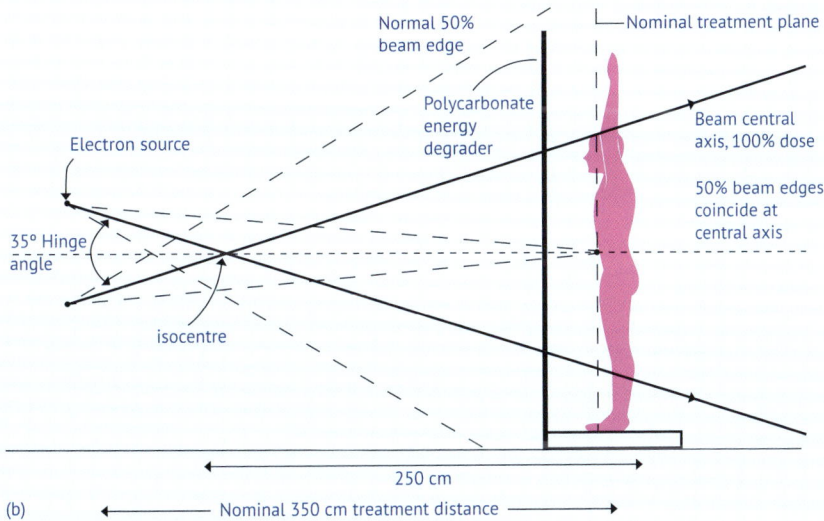

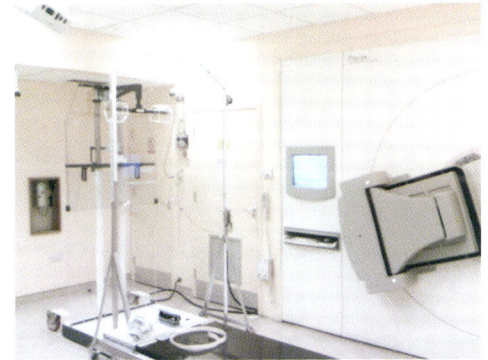

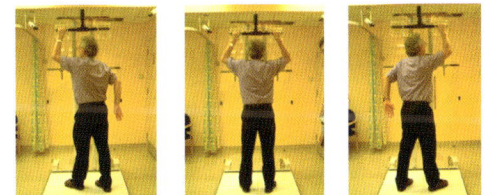

(b)

- Electron source
- 35° Hinge angle
- isocentre
- Normal 50% beam edge
- Polycarbonate energy degrader
- Nominal treatment plane
- Beam central axis, 100% dose
- 50% beam edges coincide at central axis
- 250 cm
- Nominal 350 cm treatment distance

Total Skin Electron Beam Therapy, a technique for irradiating the whole body, with a 95 per cent response rate in cutaneous lymphoma. Courtesy of Stephen Morris Consultant Clinical Oncologist who introduced TSEB to Guy's and St Thomas'.

The effect was dramatic. Within a few weeks of daily treatment, the skin cleared and patients recovered. They had to wear eye shields and lost their hair (and nails, unless they were protected). One side effect was that when hair grew back it was sometimes a different colour and texture – more like that from 30 years before.

But the main drawback was that the benefit did not last. The disease always returned – on average after 12 to 15 months. TSEB is also complex to administer – the machine must be reconfigured for each patient and the body rotated during treatment to ensure the skin gets an even dose across its surface. In the UK, St Johns is one of only three centres providing it (the others are Sheffield and Manchester).

Professor Whittaker said: "It is an extremely good palliative tool. The challenge is to maintain the response."

Using the conventional dosage, patients are limited to one treatment in their lifetime because of the toxic effect on their skin. For this reason some experts say it should be reserved for people with advanced disease.

But a new low dose regime has been devised, which involves treatment for two weeks instead of five. As it is less toxic, the treatment can be administered every five to ten years.

"It is much better tolerated so it can be repeated. We trade a bit on the duration of the response but the overall response rate is still 95 per cent," said Professor Whittaker.

New biologic drugs

Cutaneous lymphoma tends to be resistant to chemo-therapy. However, researchers are developing targeted biologic drugs that can damp down the disease.

Consultants from St John's led an international trial of the first class of drugs to target the epigenetics of the condition, which acts like a shock absorber to calm down the abnormal genes driving the lymphoma cells. Two drugs – histone deacetylase inhibitors – have been approved by the Food and Drugs Administration (FDA) in the US. They are called vorinostat and depsipeptide. But the equivalent body,

the European Medicines Agency (EMA) in the UK, has withheld a licence on the grounds that the improvement seen with the drugs is not significantly greater than with the standard treatment.

Professor Whittaker said: "We obtained a response rate of 38 per cent, with one in ten patients going into complete remission. But that was not sufficient for the EMA which claimed it was no better than the standard treatment. We say there is no standard treatment, response rates are low and we need multiple approaches. Some patients relapse early and need alternative treatments."

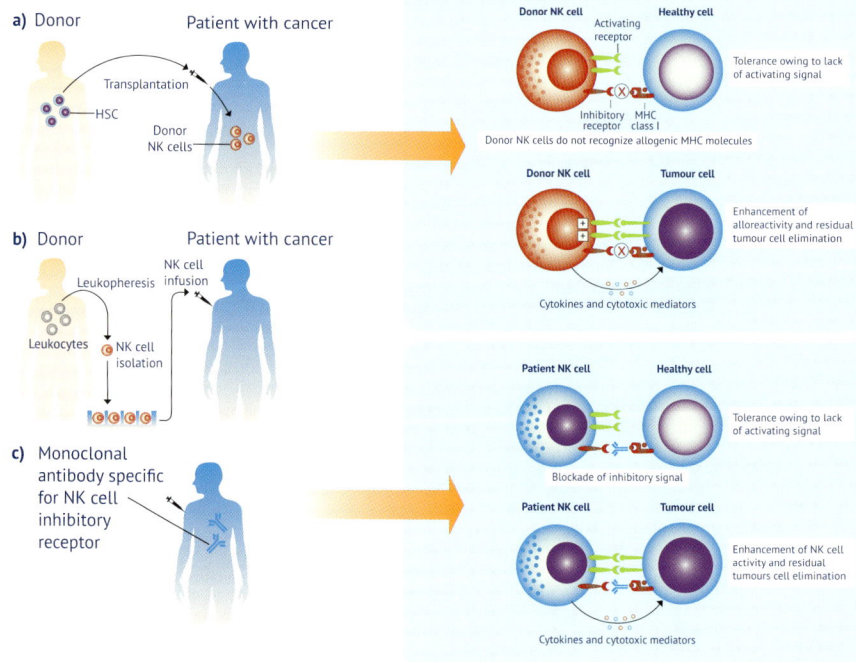

Stem Cell Transplant

For the worst affected patients, a stem cell transplant is an option. St John's has pioneered this treatment which is still in the early stages of development. The treatment places a great strain on the body so patients must be under 60 with advanced disease and fit enough to withstand it. Blood is taken from a matched donor and stem cells extracted before being infused into the patient whose own immune system is first destroyed by chemotherapy (and sometimes radiotherapy).

If successful the patient will then start producing the immune cells of the donor which will fight the lymphoma. In some patients it has been highly successful. Professor Whittaker said: "It tells us that the use of immunotherapy can work. The mechanism is not understood but in some patients the treatment has brought long term benefit. Elucidating the mechanism could help the development of future treatments."

The danger is that the new immune system may perceive the body into which it has been transplanted as "foreign" and attack it in a life-threatening condition known as "graft vs host" disease. In year one of St John's transplant programme over a third of the patients died. Today the death rate stands at 15 per cent and is continuing to come down.

St John's is collaborating with Stanford University in California, US, on developing a protocol for stem cell transplants to improve results.

Photopheresis

This is a technique, used principally for treating chronic graft vs host disease and cutaneous lymphoma, that was pioneered in the UK by St Johns in the 1980s. It involves chemically treating blood with drugs that are activated by ultraviolet light. The blood is withdrawn from the patient, treated and then re-infused – hence, the full name of the procedure: extracorporeal photopheresis.

It was originally developed at Yale University in the US as a treatment for cutaneous lymphoma where the cancer is in the blood as well as the skin. This causes abnormal blood counts and the disease looks like leukaemia.

The skin is red all over and patients suffer with

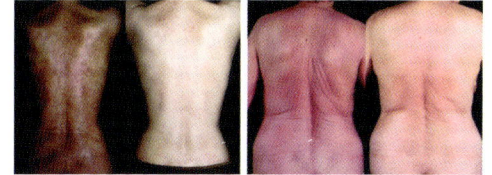

Clinical treatment effect of extracorporeal photochemotherapy showing dramatic improvement

an excruciating itch. But patients treated with the technique every four weeks showed significant clinical benefit. It is thought to switch off part of the immune system but its mechanism of action is not understood.

Between 80-90 per cent of the patients treated at St John's with the method have chronic graft vs host disease, numbering more than 100 a month.

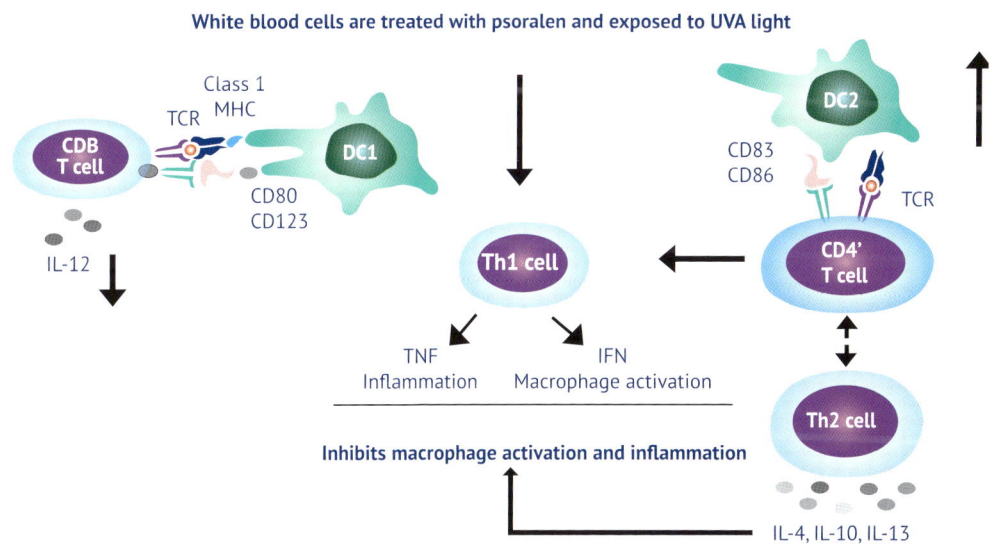

White blood cells are treated with psoralen and exposed to UVA light

CASE STUDY - **MARTIN GAMMON**

Martin Gammon, 56, knows he is living on borrowed time – thanks to a new drug that brought him back from the brink of death.

In 2005 he mentioned to his GP that he had a mole on his back which was "itching a bit". He was referred to the Queen Elizabeth hospital in Woolwich, south London, where he lived with his wife Yvonne, and was diagnosed with *melanoma*.

He was then 47. He had an operation to remove the mole and extensive tissue around it and later underwent sentinel node biopsy, the technique pioneered at St John's.

It showed a lymph gland in his neck was affected which was removed. He had a couple of years respite and then the cancer returned in the form of a growth near the missing lymph gland. It was also removed.

Another year passed but in 2010, "things went downhill". By 2011 he had been diagnosed with advanced (stage IV) melanoma.

"It was a death sentence. The doctor told me my life expectancy was three to six months. Between April and October tumours kept coming all over my body, from my legs to my head. I had 30 of them, including a brain tumour."

He had a course of chemotherapy in September 2011, but it had no effect, apart from making him feel ill. Then he and Yvonne were shopping in BHS when he got a call from St John's to say they had funding to try him on a drug, ipilimumab, a new form of immunotherapy which had just been licensed.

"I broke down and cried. It was like being offered

Martin Gammon with his late wife, Yvonne

a life raft. I said yes, I would try it."

The first of four infusions of the drug – given three weeks apart – was administered in October and the second in November. Days later Martin and Yvonne got married – they had been together for a decade but had never 'got round to it' – and left on their honeymoon, a cruise round the Mediterranean and to the US. Unfortunately, Martin fell sick in Madeira and had to be flown home where he was admitted to hospital – a reaction to the immunotherapy. As a result, he missed the third infusion but was just about well enough to have the last one on schedule in December 2011.

"After that, I got worse and worse. In January we started making plans for my funeral. I thought that was it. Then, almost overnight, I started to get better. The tumours started shrinking, including the one in my brain (as shown on a scan). By March 2012, just about everything had gone, apart from those on my liver."

In October 2012 he had an operation to remove part of his liver. Since then he has had no more treatment. Sadly, Yvonne died in 2014 but he remains well.

Nine years after being diagnosed with melanoma, he said: "I am one of the success stories. Without the drug I would have been in my grave for at least two years. It's not a miracle cure – it doesn't work for everybody. But if it works for you – that is what counts."

The future

The basic research undertaken at St Johns is allied closely to patients needs. "It is not about stitching mice together," said Professor Whittaker.

Genes hold the key. Examining the genetic make-up of tumours for abnormalities and the prevalence of the mutations across a population is a major area of research for the future. There may be half a dozen genes that are important but establishing whether they are a necessary cause of the disease, or connected with each other, is the challenge.

Professor Whittaker said: "There has been little improvement in survival in 25 years but there are big potential gains on the horizon. We are caring for our patients better mainly due to the excellent compassionate care provided by our wonderful team of specialist skin cancer clinical nurse specialists and working to develop a more targeted approach to treatment based on tumour genome sequencing. That promises the next leap forward."

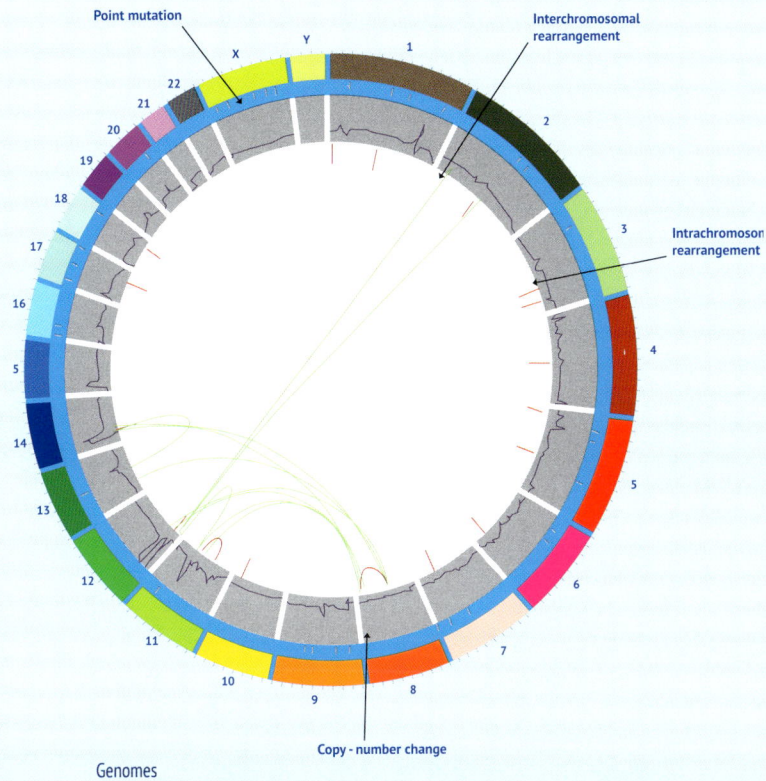

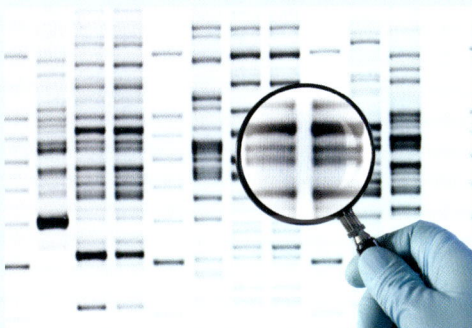

Point mutation

Interchromosomal rearrangement

Intrachromosomal rearrangement

Copy - number change

Genomes

Genetic screening

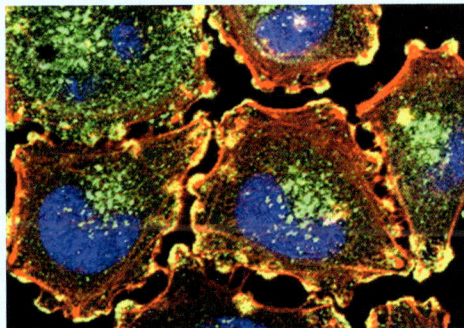

Melanoma cell

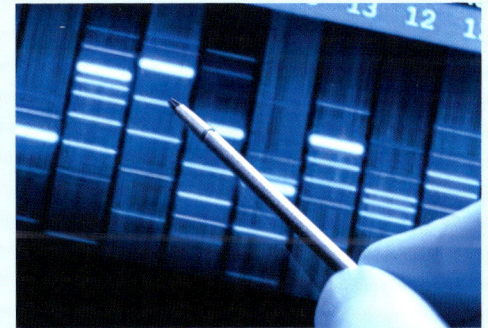

Human Genome sequencing

SKIN AND THE IMMUNE SYSTEM

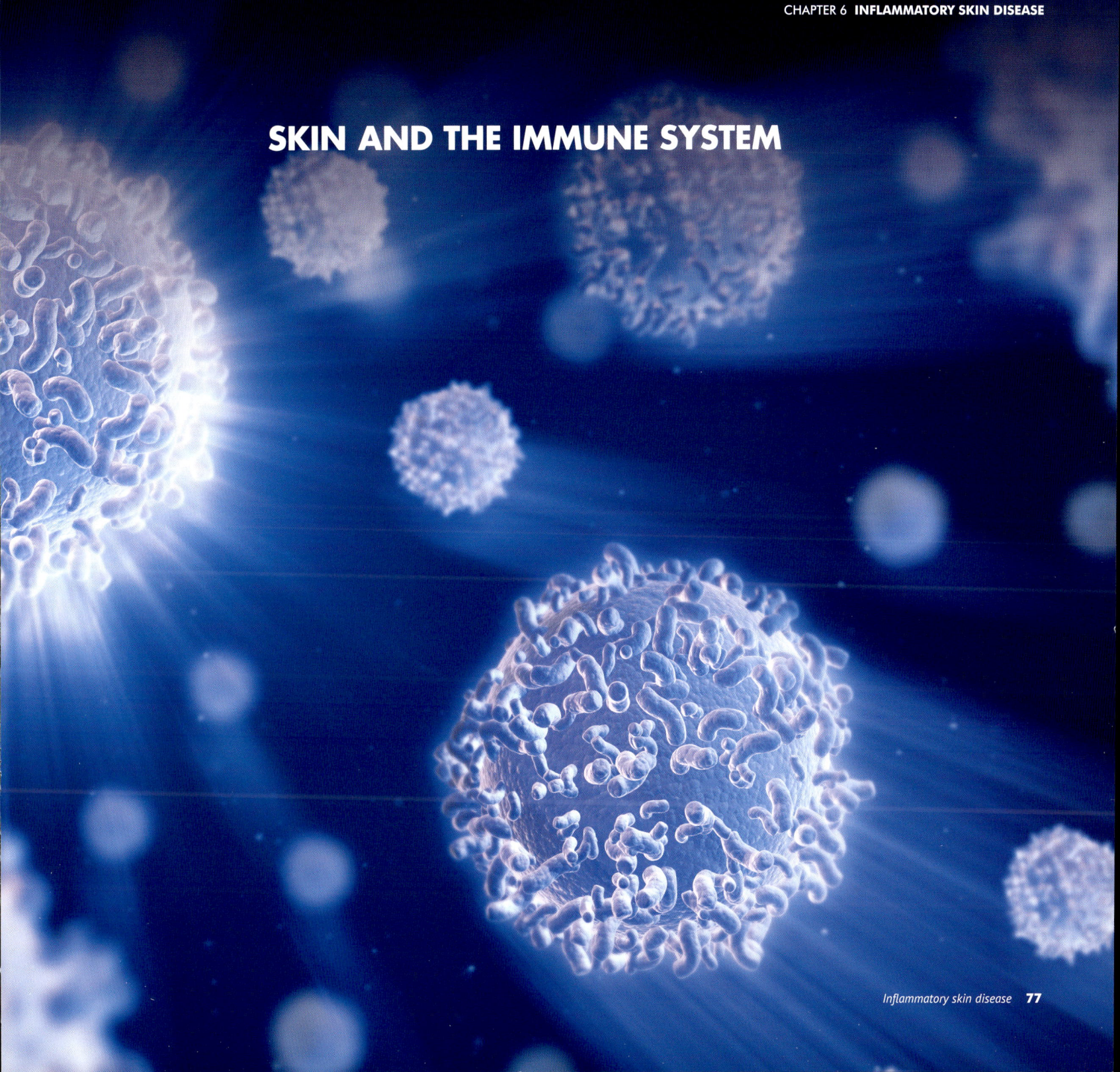

Psoriasis

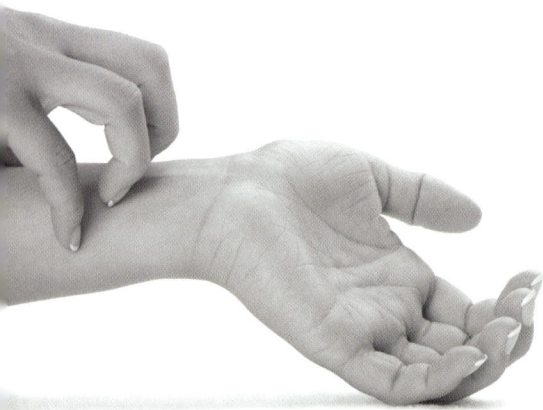

Inflammatory skin disease forms a major component of dermatology – which includes the red and scaly condition psoriasis, the itchy weals of urticaria and the blistering skin disorders of immuno-bullous disease.

Psoriasis is the most common – affecting one in 50 of the population worldwide, more than one million in the UK. The best known sufferer is still fictional hero Philip Marlow, the louche, cynical mystery writer and star of Dennis Potter's BBC TV series "The Singing Detective", broadcast in 1986.

Hospitalised by severe psoriasis and psoriatic arthritis, creamed, bandaged and feverish, Marlow falls into a fantasy world in which the hospital, the noir thriller and wartime England merge. The series was voted the 20th best all time TV programme by the British Film Institute in 2000. Potter was himself a lifelong sufferer from psoriasis and psoriatic arthritis - and was treated at St Johns. Like Marlow, he was an awkward patient.

St John's runs one of the major tertiary services for severe psoriasis in the country (the other is in Manchester). Although the condition is common, a minority have severe disease accounting for 10-20 per cent of the total. It is caused by the skin cells being replaced too quickly, the product of an over-active immune system. Normally skin cells take three to four weeks to replace themselves but in psoriasis they take less than a week.

The mainstay of treatment for most sufferers is creams and ointments to soothe and moisturise the red, scaly and cracked skin that may become sore and painful. Until a decade ago Dithranol, and also crude coal tar, applied directly to the psoriatic plaques as a paste was a mainstay treatment but because it could burn normal skin it had to be applied in hospital by trained nurses and required a stay of two to three weeks.

Psoriasis – from the Greek word psora meaning itch – was known as the "antidote to the dermatologist's ego". Severe cases would spend weeks in hospital or were treated with immunosuppressants such as ciclosporin and methotrexate, to damp down over-active immune systems. These drugs are still used but are only effective in some patients and occasionally have serious side effects. Methotrexate is linked with problems of the bone marrow and liver and patients require regular monitoring.

At the turn of the millennium there was a dramatic change. The introduction of the new biologic drugs, custom designed to target specific parts of the immune system, has transformed the outlook for patients severely affected with psoriasis. At St John's the first patient was infused with the drug infliximab, a monoclonal antibody, in 2001.

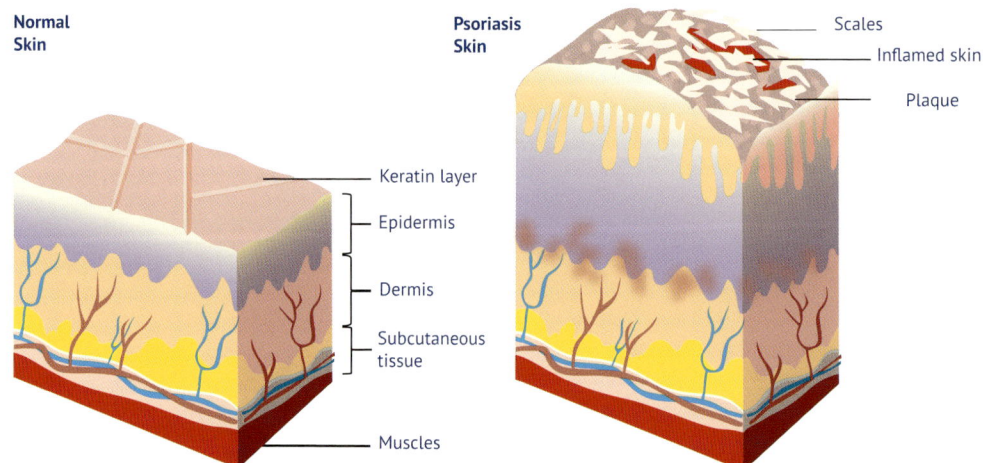

Normal Skin — Keratin layer, Epidermis, Dermis, Subcutaneous tissue, Muscles

Psoriasis Skin — Scales, Inflamed skin, Plaque

More than one million people are affected by psoriasis in the UK of whom 10-20 per cent have severe disease

The psoriasis team at St John's: there has been an 80 per cent reduction in in-patient episodes

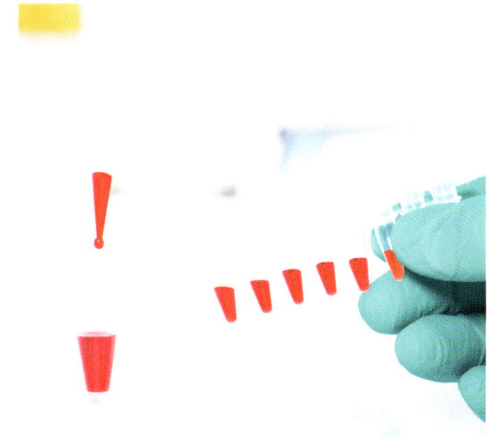

Several biologic drugs are now available

Three more biologics have since become available – *ustekinumab*, the most recent, can be self-injected by the patient just three to four times a year.

Professor **Catherine Smith**, consultant dermatologist, said: "People with *psoriasis* used to come in and out of hospital. Now we have had an 80 per cent reduction in in-patient episodes. These drugs are life-transforming. Almost 70 per cent of patients on treatment are clear or near clear."

She added: "Some patients comment that they almost forget they have psoriasis."

Before the advent of the biologic drugs, doctors struggled with the most severely affected patients in an attempt to make their lives bearable. Searching for a treatment that worked, they used multiple immunosuppressants in combination to increase the drugs' impact – but at the risk of over-suppressing the patient's immune system leaving them vulnerable to a serious infection.

Psoriasis is not fatal but in its worst manifestation it is so severe that sufferers cannot function.

Powerful immunosuppressants were used in severe cases of psoriasis, and sometimes still are. But the new biologic drugs have transformed the outlook for patients

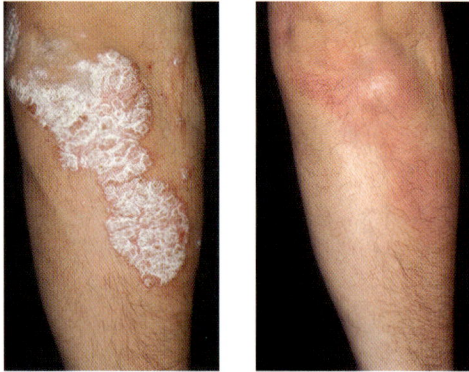
Psoriasis plaque before and after treatment

Although the new biologic drugs are very effective, they do not help all patients, and they are costly

Professor **Jonathan Barker**, consultant dermatologist, said: "It is socially disfiguring. Having a partner, wearing dark suits, going swimming are all problematic. Physically the skin is sore and weeping and if the hands and feet are affected they can't work or walk. There is a high incidence of depression, and also in some patients alcohol misuse in order to cope."

Those days are now past for many patients with severe disease. If Dennis Potter was alive today he and his fictional alter ego would have a very different outlook.

But there is a downside. While the drugs leave most patients clear or near clear (70 per cent) – that leaves many still not helped. And much depends on which areas of the skin are clear. If sensitive areas such as the face remain affected then the impact of the drug is greatly diminished. Complete clearance of the condition is achieved in only half of patients.

Professor Smith said: "Expectations have been raised. But at least 30 per cent of patients are not helped and 50 per cent are not fully clear. That is a problem."

Even in those who have a good response, some will fail later. Some suffer side effects – these are powerful drugs. Around 15 per cent stop responding after a year, and this is ongoing, year by year. The drugs are also most effective in *plaque-type psoriasis*, much less so – if at all – in other types such as *pustular psoriasis*.

Finally, there is the question of cost. The drugs are expensive, at around £10,000 per patient per year and St John's has around 400 currently taking them. They consume 60 per cent of NHS spending on *psoriasis* therapies though they help only a minority of patients.

This underlines the need for further research. A consortium of institutions, including St John's, has won a £7 million grant from the Medical Research Council to investigate the best way of prescribing

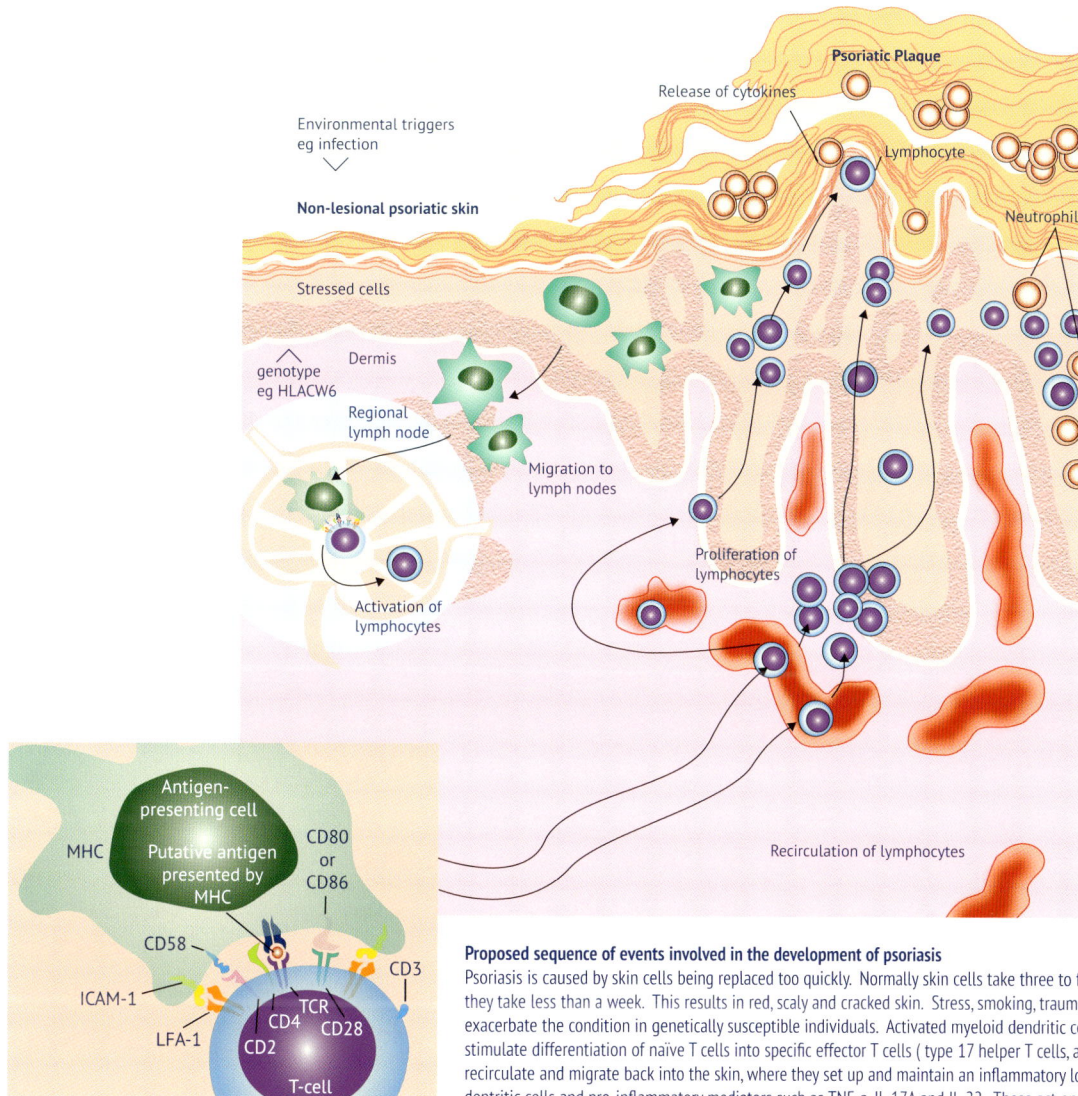

Psoriatic Plaque

Release of cytokines

Lymphocyte

Environmental triggers
eg infection

Neutrophils

Non-lesional psoriatic skin

Stressed cells

genotype
eg HLACW6

Dermis

Regional
lymph node

Migration to
lymph nodes

Proliferation of
lymphocytes

Activation of
lymphocytes

Recirculation of lymphocytes

Antigen-
presenting cell

MHC

Putative antigen
presented by
MHC

CD80
or
CD86

CD58

CD3

ICAM-1

TCR
CD4   CD28
CD2

LFA-1

T-cell

Proposed sequence of events involved in the development of psoriasis
Psoriasis is caused by skin cells being replaced too quickly. Normally skin cells take three to four weeks to replace themselves but in psoriasis they take less than a week. This results in red, scaly and cracked skin. Stress, smoking, trauma and infection are among the triggers that can exacerbate the condition in genetically susceptible individuals. Activated myeloid dendritic cells migrate to draining lymph nodes and stimulate differentiation of naïve T cells into specific effector T cells (type 17 helper T cells, and type 1 helper T cells). These T cells then recirculate and migrate back into the skin, where they set up and maintain an inflammatory loop, driven by release of IL-23 from dermal dentritic cells and pro-inflammatory mediators such as TNF-a, IL-17A and IL-22. These act on keratinocytes which also drive inflammation and further cell recruitment (eg: neutrophils).

the new drugs. The Psoriasis Stratification to Optimise Relevant Therapy (PSORT) project is designed to identify the markers that will enable doctors to target treatments more effectively. These may be genetic, immunological, pharmacological (for example, the best dosing regime) or clinical.

"The aim is to get the right dose into the right patient at the right time," said Professor Barker.

Much is known about the genetic and immunological mechanisms underlying the pathogenesis of *psoriasis* and the key role of tumour necrosis factor, an immune system mediator. In 2009, researchers at St John's, together with their collaborators, uncovered genetic evidence to explain the mechanism of action of the biologic drugs, which had up till then been used on a trial and error basis. Their paper, published in Nature Genetics, revealed the specific parts of the immune system that are involved in causing psoriasis including the IL-17 pathway. The discovery represented a key piece of the jigsaw in the search for new treatments.

Professor Barker said: "Our genetic research delineated exactly how and why the biologics work. Drug development can now proceed in a targeted way. It is science-led as opposed to being driven by serendipity."

The breakthrough underlined the importance of having researchers working with patients on the wards, something St John's prides itself on.

Professor Barker said: "The unique thing about St John's is that researchers and clinicians collaborate together. Having clinical academics with joint appointments at the Trust [Guy's and St Thomas'] and the university [King's College London] means they can do patient-based research. True collaboration of this kind is very unusual. As a result, St John's can provide state of the art treatment for patients with severe disease, high quality teaching for clinicians as well as conducting cutting edge research."

Professor Smith added: "You need to see what is happening to the patients as a researcher so you can go back to the lab and make adjustments. Involvement of clinicians and patients with clinical research ensures the right research questions are being asked."

Professor Smith chaired a scientific panel of the National Institute for Health and Care Excellence (NICE) that produced the first guideline for health care professionals on the management of psoriasis in 2012 – another illustration of the influence of St John's.

Immuno-bullous disorder

There are many types of blistering skin disease, some of which are caused by the body's immune system attacking the proteins that bind the skin cells in the epidermis (the outer layer) and that also attach the epidermis to the dermis (inner layer). These proteins are in effect the glue that holds the skin together - when damaged the layers separate and a blister forms.

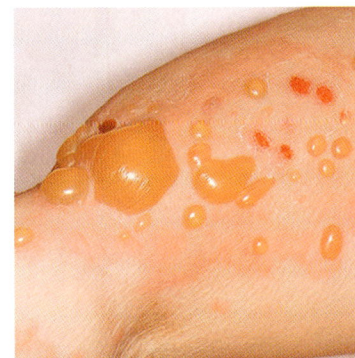

Bullous pemphigoid

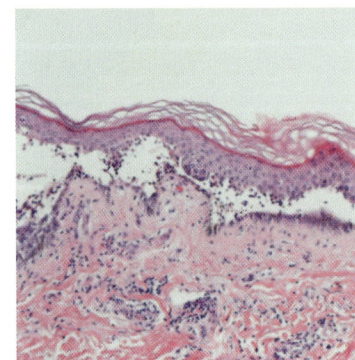

Pemphigus vulgaris

Bullous pemphigoid: a blistering skin disease caused by the body's immune system attacking the proteins that bind the epidermis (outer layer) to the dermis (inner layer). When damaged, the layers separate and a blister forms.

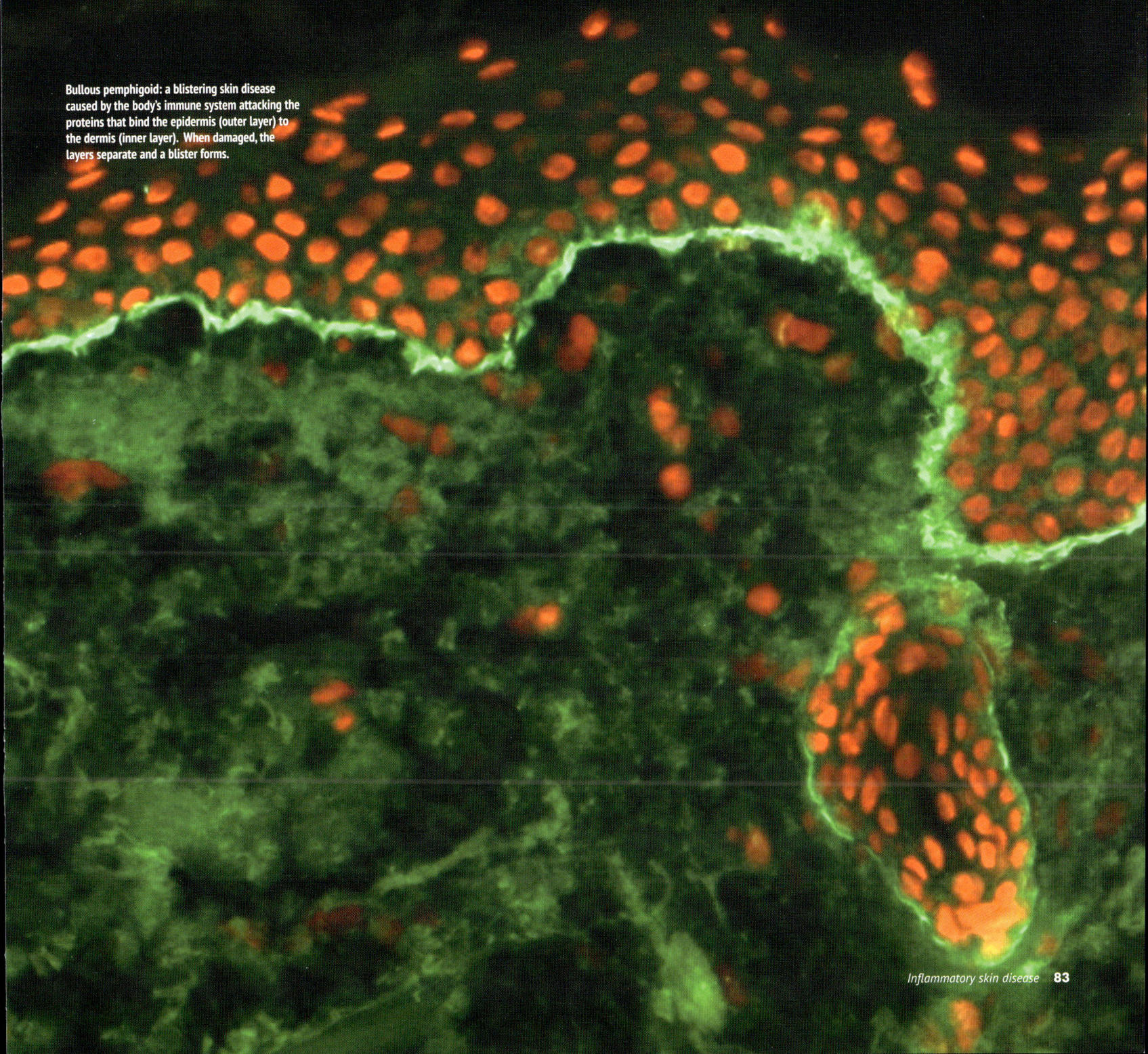

Immunobullous diseases are uncommon but potentially serious disorders that result in blisters affecting all parts of the skin, the eyes, mouth and genitalia. In the past, before steroid treatment became available, patients would

Martin Black

often die from overwhelming infection and fluid loss through the skin.

The commonest types of immunobullous disease are *pemphigus*, which causes raw sores in the mouth and blisters on the skin, and *pemphigoid* which is associated with deep blisters appearing at the junction between the epidermis and underlying dermis.

The conditions can be difficult to diagnose because many other diseases also cause blistering, and must be excluded.

St John's runs the UK's largest clinical service for the disorder, which is highly regarded in part because diagnosis, treatment and research are brought together in one department.

"The laboratory is an integral part of the service. We do not have to send biopsies away to be examined. Pathology is not separate so we can relate the clinical signs to the appearance of the specimen on the slide. That is significant for outcomes and for research," said consultant Dr **Richard Groves**.

The department has led research into prognostic biomarkers for the disease, thanks to the creation of a biobank of blood samples from patients built up over an unparalleled 20 years thanks to the foresight of Professor **Martin Black** who set up the IMF lab.

Chronic Urticaria

Chronic urticaria is a condition where an itchy nettlerash comes and goes daily or almost daily for at least six weeks. It is often accompanied by deeper swellings called angio-oedema. Patients feel unwell when it is severe and find it difficult to sleep because of the irritation.

It is distinguished from *acute urticaria* which typically develops suddenly and unexpectedly. It may follow a viral infection but the cause of many cases remains unknown. It is often believed that allergy is responsible but it is unusual to find a specific food, drug or sting trigger. The illness may last up to 6 weeks but usually resolves over a few days.

Acute urticaria is common – about one in six people will have at least one bout during their life and it can strike at any age. *Chronic urticaria* is less common affecting one in 1000 people and in some cases can last for years. It may be very disabling for some patients and result in problems with employment, education and self-esteem.

Urticaria is caused by the release of histamine and other inflammatory substances from mast cells in the skin in response to a trigger. Often the trigger is unidentified - until 25 years ago it was known as *chronic idiopathic urticaria* – of "unknown cause". Today the term *chronic spontaneous urticaria* is preferred because the cause can be found in some patients.

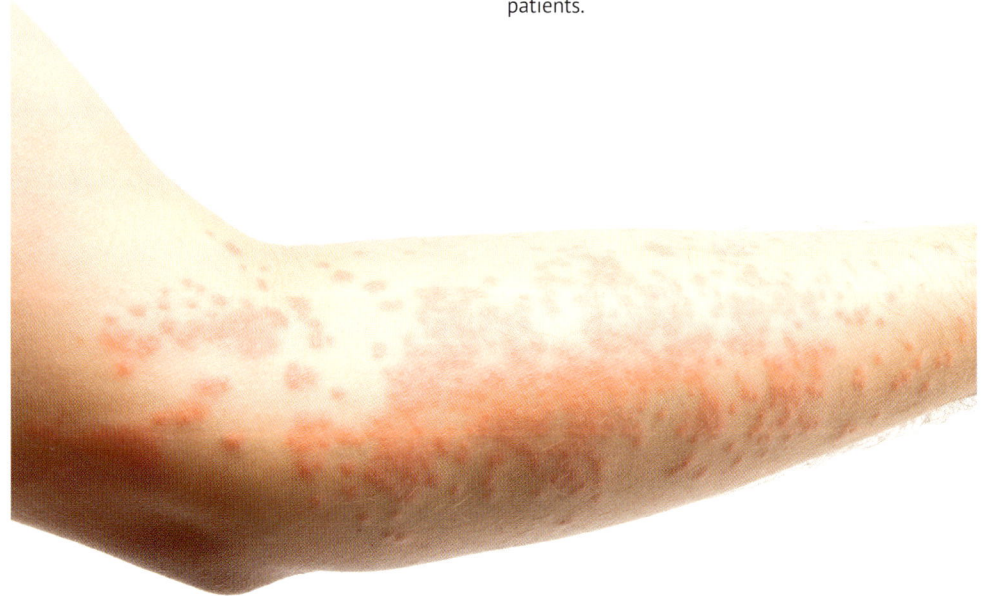

Chronic urticaria affects one in 1,000 people causing an itchy nettlerash often accompanied by deeper swellings

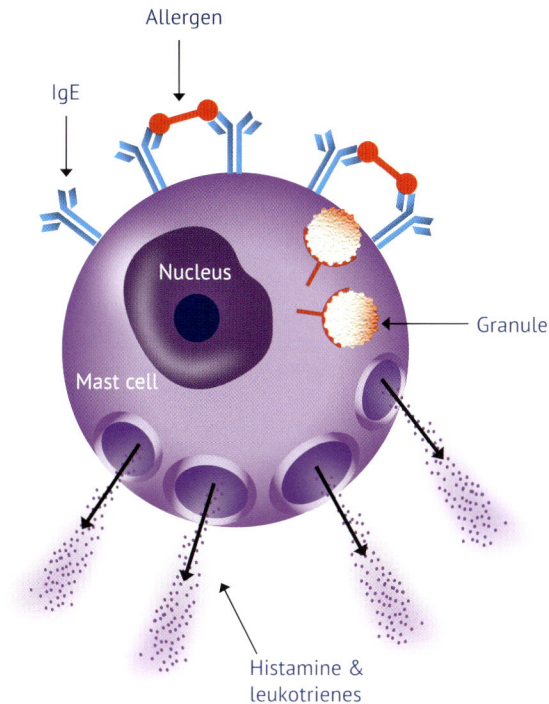

The release of histamine causes fluid to leak from the tiny blood vessels under the skin forming itchy red weals.

Malcolm Greaves

Clive Grattan

The release of histamine causes fluid to leak from the tiny blood vessels under the skin which collects to form itchy red weals. In half of cases, anti-histamines provide at least partial relief.

The worst affected patients may develop *angio-oedema* – swelling of the tissues. If the swelling affects the throat and breathing becomes difficult, emergency treatment is required with an injection of adrenaline.

In the 1990s, Professor **Malcolm Greaves** and **Clive Grattan** of St John's uncovered the mechanism that underlies around 30 per cent of patients with *chronic spontaneous urticaria*. They isolated and described the antibodies circulating in the blood that triggered IgE and its receptors on the mast cells leading to the release of histamine.

The discovery marked a paradigm shift in understanding the disease and led to the realisation that up to 30 per cent of patients with *chronic spontaneous urticaria* in fact have *autoimmune chronic urticaria*. The diagnosis was important because it carried implications for the appropriate treatment.

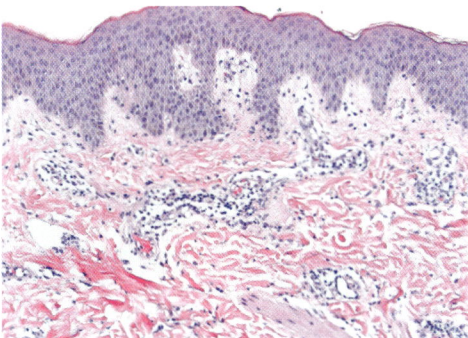

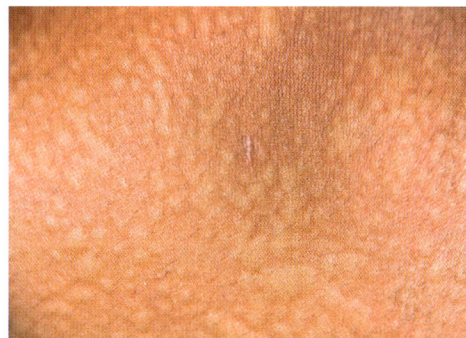

In the 1990s the mechanism that underlies 30 per cent of cases of chronic spontaneous urticaria was uncovered at St John's

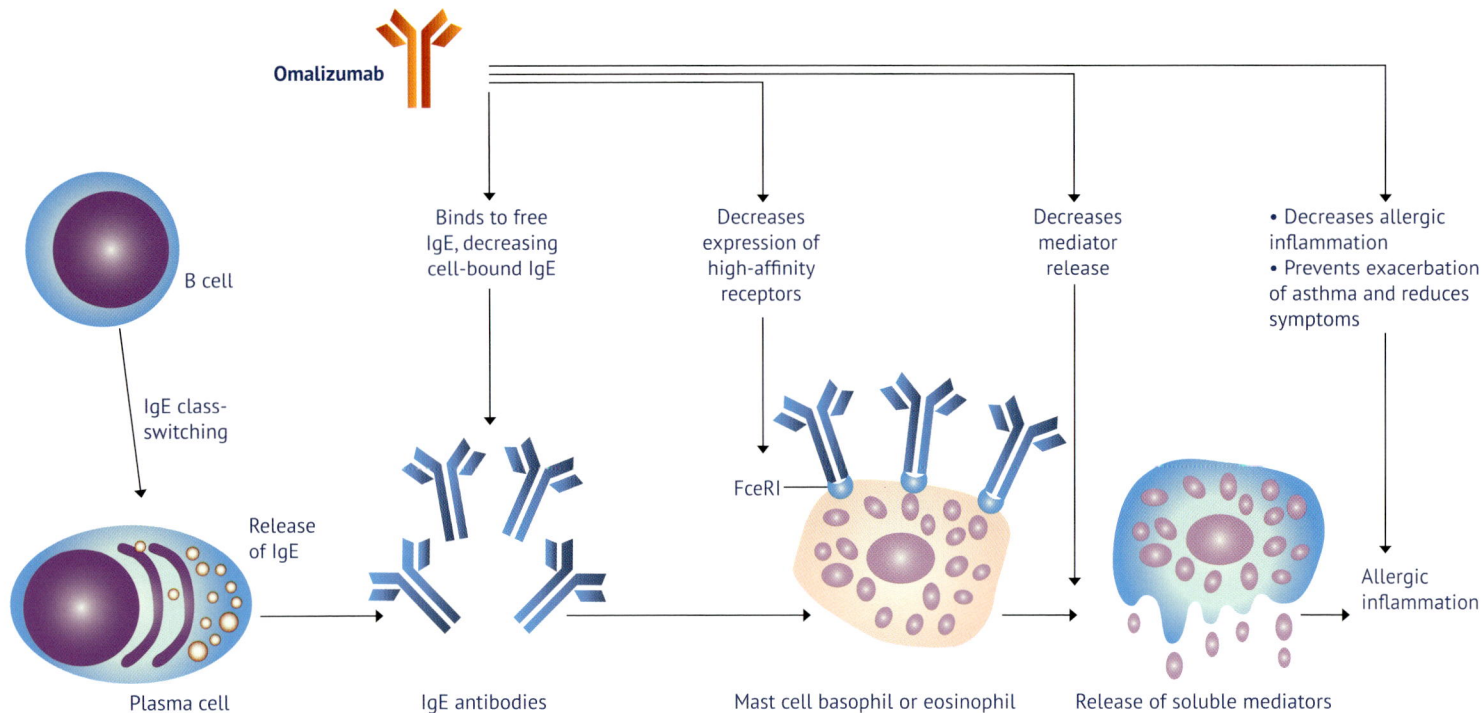

Omalizumab

B cell

IgE class-switching

Release of IgE

Plasma cell

Binds to free IgE, decreasing cell-bound IgE

Decreases expression of high-affinity receptors

Decreases mediator release

• Decreases allergic inflammation
• Prevents exacerbation of asthma and reduces symptoms

FceRI

IgE antibodies

Mast cell basophil or eosinophil

Release of soluble mediators

Allergic inflammation

Omalizumab: the first biologic drug to be licensed in the UK for chronic urticaria can be life changing for patients with severe disease

For people with *chronic urticaria* who do not respond to anti-histamines, the treatment options have been few. More severe cases are treated with immunosuppressants such as *ciclosporin* or *methotrexate*. Some patients have needed steroids to control their condition.

Now a monoclonal antibody, *omalizumab*, which has been used for a decade to treat severe asthma, is the first biologic drug to be licensed in the UK and Europe for the treatment of *chronic urticaria* (March 2014). It probably works, at least in part, by preventing the autoantibodies, identifed by Prof Greaves and Grattan, from binding to mast cells

Professor **Clive Grattan** said: "This can be a life changing drug for patients with severe, intractable disease."

Some patients at St John's are already having it. But like the other biologics, *omalizumab* is expensive.

Women's Dermatology Service

Some skin diseases, such as *lichen sclerosus*, specifically target the genital region. Others can affect the genitalia as well as other parts of the body, but because the vulva is a sensitive body site, with thinner and more vulnerable skin, it requires different treatment. As these women have specific needs, both physical and psychological, a separate service was developed at St Johns for them in the early 1990s. [An equivalent service for men is offered at the Chelsea and Westminster Hospital, London.]

It was the brainchild of **Marjorie Ridley**, consultant dermatologist, who established the first clinic for the diagnosis and treatment of genital dermatoses at the Elizabeth Garrett Anderson hospital in the 1970s and published a textbook 'The Vulva."(1975). After retiring in 1991, she became an honorary consultant at St John's and helped establish the vulval clinic.

Dr **Fiona Lewis** said: "In the past, some women underwent extensive and unnecessary surgery for genital dermatoses. Marjorie's contribution was to emphasise the importance of early dermatological diagnosis and promote a more rational approach to treatment. She was also important in helping educate dermatologists, gynaecologists and other specialists about vulval disorders."

Marjorie Ridley

A separate service for women was established in the 1990s

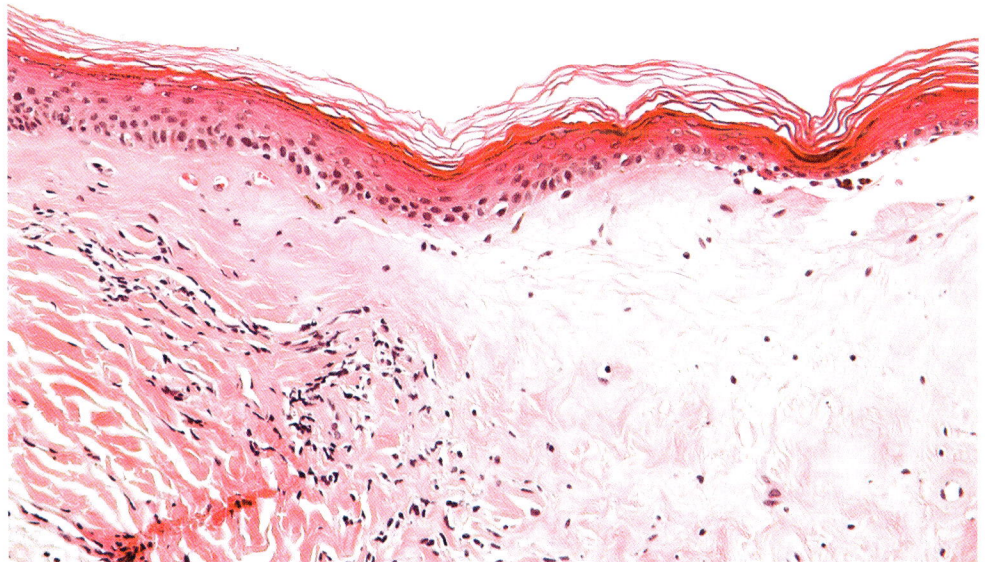

Lichen sclerosus targets the genital region and led in the past to unnecessary surgery

Hidradenitis suppurativa

Hidradenitis suppurativa (HS) is a painful long term condition that causes abscesses and scarring on the skin. It is a disease of the skin carrying the apocrine (sweat) glands that principally affects the armpits and groin area but can extend to the buttocks, lower abdomen, chest and neck. It can be associated with severe acne, arthritis and inflammatory bowel disease.

An estimated 1 per cent of the population is affected though people are often too embarrassed to seek help.

The disease ranges from mild to severe. Dr **Nemesha Desai,** clinical lead of the HS service said: "Patients with severe disease have very difficult lives with recurrent painful boils and malodorous wounds that chronically discharge pus. They may be subjected to disfiguring surgery to remove the abnormal skin and replace it with grafts from other areas and require treatment with long term antibiotics and immunosuppressive therapy. There is a huge unmet need."

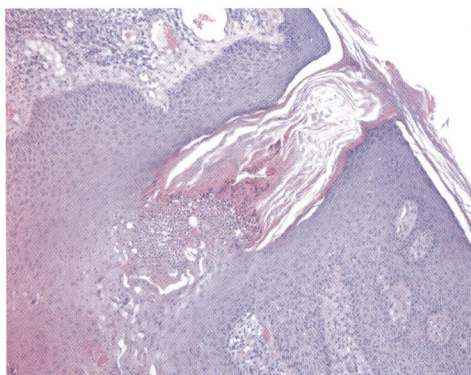

Keratin plug
Hair folicle
Apocrine gland
Fistula
Abscess
Bacteria

(1) Keratin plug blocks hair follicle
(2) Bacteria multiply in apocrine gland
(3) Apocrine gland bursts releasing bacteria
(4) Secondary bacterial infection leads to abscess formation
(5) Abscess drains creating fistulous tract
(6) Healing leads to scarring and fibrosis of skin

Hidradenitis suppurativa is a disease of the skin carrying the sweat glands and principally affects the armpits (above and below) and the groin

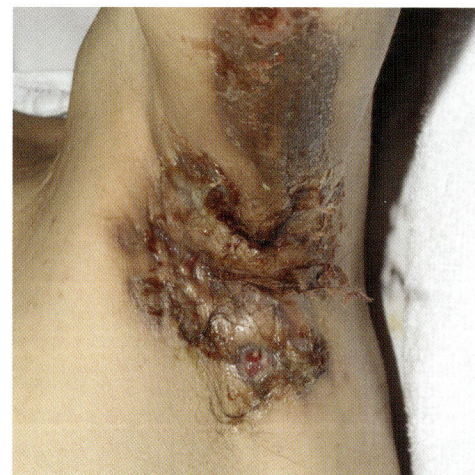

Hidradenitis suppurativa: causes abscesses

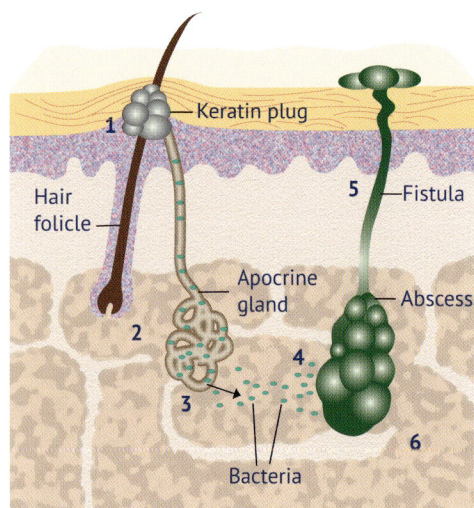

St John's has taken the pioneering step of establishing the first tertiary referral service for *hidradenitis suppurativa* in the UK. It is a multidisciplinary service set up in 2010 by Nemesha Desai, consultant dermatologist. The team includes specialists from other services such as plastic surgery, gastroenterology and colorectal surgeons, who are involved in the management of HS and related conditions such as inflammatory bowel disease. The HS Service has an active research interest, working closely with the Skin Therapy Research Unit at Kings College London investigating the genetic basis of the condition.

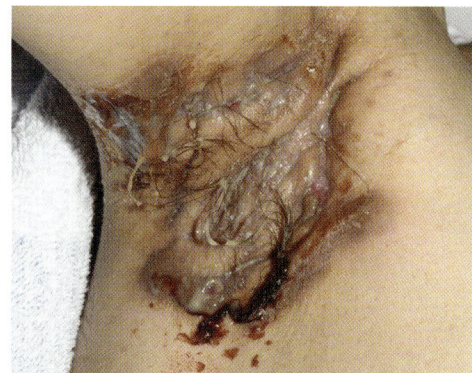

CASE STUDY - **JOHN WEST**

As a teenager growing up with psoriasis in the 1960s, John West suffered twice – once from the condition and secondly from the reaction people had to it. Aged 16, following an operation, the disease flared and became very acute.

John West: "To have a drug that cleared my psoriasis has been absolutely wonderful."

"It was all over my body. It affected me very badly. I couldn't go swimming or play football – it was changing with other people, that was the embarrassing part."

Treatments at that time consisted of creams and lotions. Coal tar lotion was an important stand-by but it was messy, stained clothes (and hospital floors) and made patients "smell like a motorway".

Nothing was effective. There was no choice but to learn to live with it. "In winter you knew your skin would become red, sore, cracked and bleeding. You knew it was coming – it was unpleasant to contemplate."

That was how things stood for most of John's adult life. He got married, had children and pursued a career in business.

In the 1990s he was given a trial of *ciclosporin*, the immunosuppressant prescribed for transplant patients to prevent rejection of a new organ.

"*Ciclosporin* was 70 per cent effective, which for someone in my condition was fantastic. But it affected my kidneys and liver and my consultant had to take me off it – much to my annoyance."

Then in 2006, he was asked if he wanted to participate in a trial of a new drug, a monocolonal antibody called *ustekinumab*, which helps regulate over-active immune systems.

"Within a few weeks my *psoriasis* started getting better. You could almost watch it improve by the hour. And that is the way it has remained

for the past seven years. All that is left are a few patches on my elbows and knees."

Today, aged 66, he runs an exhibition company, lives in Maidstone, Kent and comes up to St John's every three months for an injection of the drug.

"I have not looked back since. My grandchildren – the eldest is 9 – have never known their grandad with funny skin. I have had absolutely no side effects. That is what is remarkable. It has allowed me to go swimming and I have joined a gym."

"To have a drug that cleared my *psoriasis* has been absolutely wonderful. It has completely changed my life."

OUR TOXIC WORLD: THE CAUSES OF ALLERGY

The number of people with a skin sensitivity to substances ranging from cosmetics to household products, substances at work and in the general environment runs into the millions. One in five of the population is "atopic" – with a tendency to develop eczema, hay fever or asthma – and is liable to develop rashes, weals and other skin reactions from contact with products including perfumes, hair dyes and costume jewellery.

In these circumstances, the most effective intervention may not be that delivered in the clinic but that secured in Whitehall and Westminster. Changes to public health policy have spared many more people from the pain and discomfort of skin allergy than the treatments and medicaments prescribed by doctors and nurses.

St John's has been in the forefront of campaigns to secure these changes and has been instrumental in protecting populations across Europe from exposure to substances liable to inflame and irritate the skin.

In December 2013, *Cosmetics Europe*, the European Cosmetics Trade Association, called on its members to stop using the chemical methylisothiazolinone (MI) in certain products after a review committee of the European Commission, chaired by a St John's dermatologist, **Ian White**, urged it be banned.

The move followed an explosion of allergic reactions among users since the chemical, a preservative to extend shelf life, was added to cosmetics from 2005.

Dr White, head of the department of Cutaneous Allergy at St John's, said: "The frequency of reactions to MI is unprecedented in my experience.

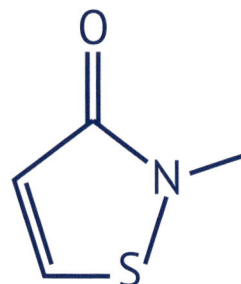

Methylisothiazolinone, a preservative used in cosmetics to extend shelf life since 2005

Contact allergy to this permitted preservative is of epidemic proportions. We have never seen anything quite like it."

The victory is the latest in the constant struggle to keep consumers safe from new substances – and sometimes old ones – to which they may have allergic reactions. Products from hair dyes to perfumes have been re-formulated, against intense opposition from the industries involved, to make them less harmful for customers to use.

The introduction of methylisothiazolinone into cosmetics, perfumes and hair dyes led to an explosion in allergic reactions

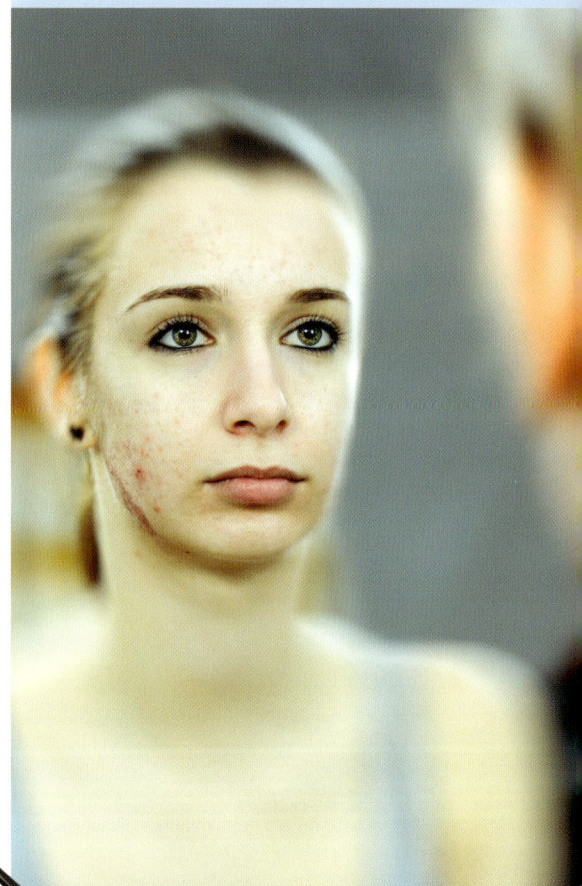

In December 2013, Cosmetics Europe called on its members to stop using methylisothiazolinone, a victory for a St John's-led campaign

Types of allergy

When a patient arrives at the St John's Cutaneous Allergy department for investigation of their eczema, they will be tested for their sensitivity to a range of contact allergens. The key to effective management of allergic diseases is making an accurate diagnosis and identifying the substance(s) responsible. Allergy testing is a crucial part of this.

Once the cause is identified, counselling and advice on how to avoid the offending substance will help reduce or eliminate symptoms and use of medication, and improve quality of life.

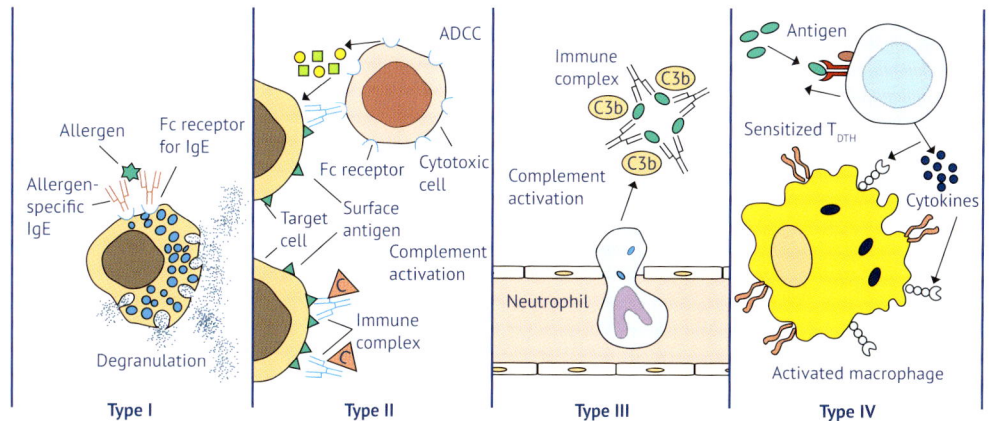

Four types of allergic reaction

Asthma

Hay fever

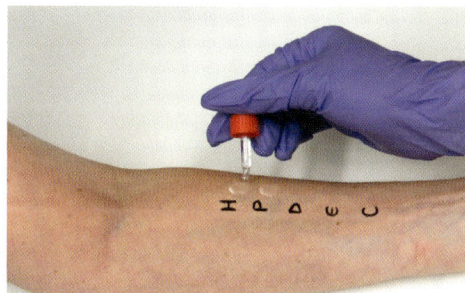

Dust mites

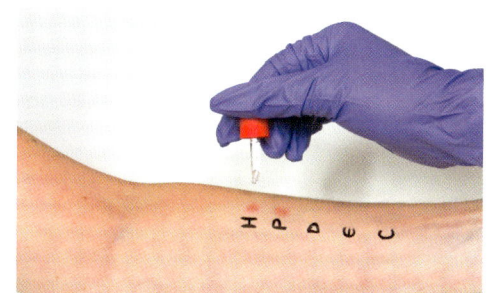

Urticaria

Skin prick test - application

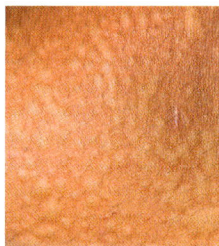

Skin prick test - reaction

There are four types of allergic reaction, two of which are particularly important for the skin. Type 1 (immediate) sensitivity is evaluated by skin prick testing and involves making a series of tiny punctures into the skin through which suspected allergens are introduced such as pollen, grass, house dust mite proteins, peanut extract and so on. If the person is allergic a visible inflammatory reaction, like a mosquito bite, will appear in 10-20 minutes.

This technique is used for identifying allergens that may cause *asthma* or *hayfever* as well as skin reactions such as *urticaria*. **The Type 1 reaction** is IgE-mediated and involves the stimulation of mast cells to release histamine causing the weals which characteristically appear on the skin. This will be dealt with more fully in Chapter Six: Inflammatory Skin Disease.

The Type 2 Cytotoxic Antibody Reaction is the blood group incompatibility that causes transfusion reactions - it does not involve the skin.

The Type 3 Immune Complex Reaction is seen in reactions to certain drugs, and may cause vasculitis with inflammation of small blood vessels in the skin.

The key allergy involving the skin, which will be discussed here, is **Type 4 cell-mediated delayed hypersensitivity**, which involves T-lymphocytes.

This is what lies behind common allergies such as that to chemicals in perfume, hair dyes, preservatives, resins, rubber and metals – in costume jewellery and coins – also known as *allergic contact dermatitis*.

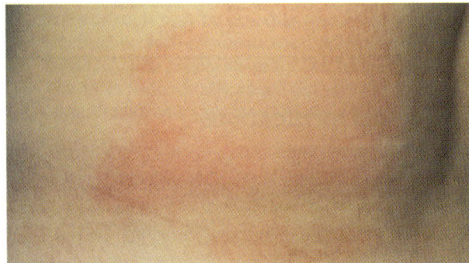
Patch testing – the Finn Chamber technique

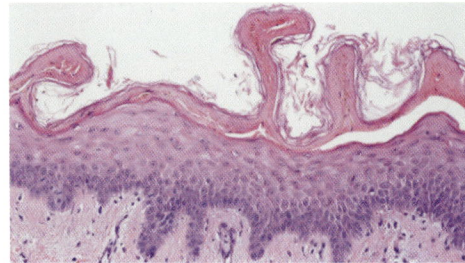
Weal - urticaria

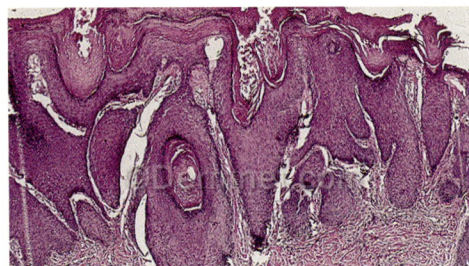
Irritant contact dermatitis

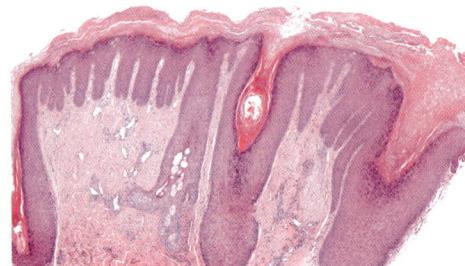
Eczema - histology

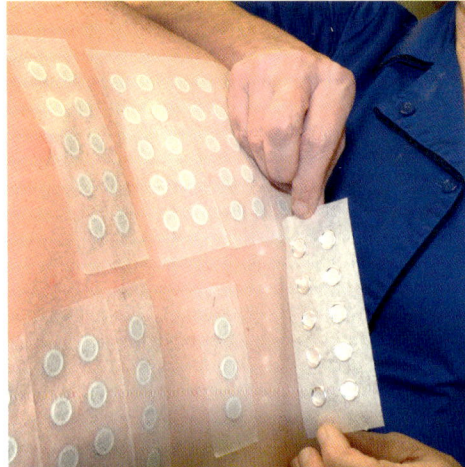
Hyperkeratosis

Patch testing

The fundamental method for identifying Type 4 allergy is patch testing. This is designed to reveal whether the patient has a specific allergy to a substance that comes into contact with their skin and may be the cause of their skin inflammation

Common allergens such as sunscreens, hair dyes and medicaments, together with other relevant chemical substances, are applied to small aluminium discs the size of a five pence piece and applied in rows to the skin, usually on the upper back, for 48 hours.

Known as the Finn Chamber technique, it tells the dermatologist whether the individual has a contact allergy to the substances being tested.

Dr White, consultant dermatologist and head of the cutaneous allergy clinic, said:

"Patch testing is one of the few ways of objectively investigating eczema. You can demonstrate the presence or absence of an allergic factor relevant to their condition. Fundamentally you are exposing individuals under standardised conditions to the suspected allergen. Then it is up to the clinician to interpret the significance of the finding."

Patch testing was introduced to St John's in the 1950s by **Charles Calnan**, then a registrar at the hospital who later rose to head the Institute as the University of London's first Professor of Dermatology.

He specialised in *contact dermatitis* and was appointed consultant in 1956 before being promoted to professor in 1961. He started keeping photographic records of all skin conditions treated at St John's and built up the world class skin allergy testing unit that exists today. He was the first editor

Patch testing was introduced at St John's in
the 1950s. It is still one of the few ways of
investigating potential causes of eczema

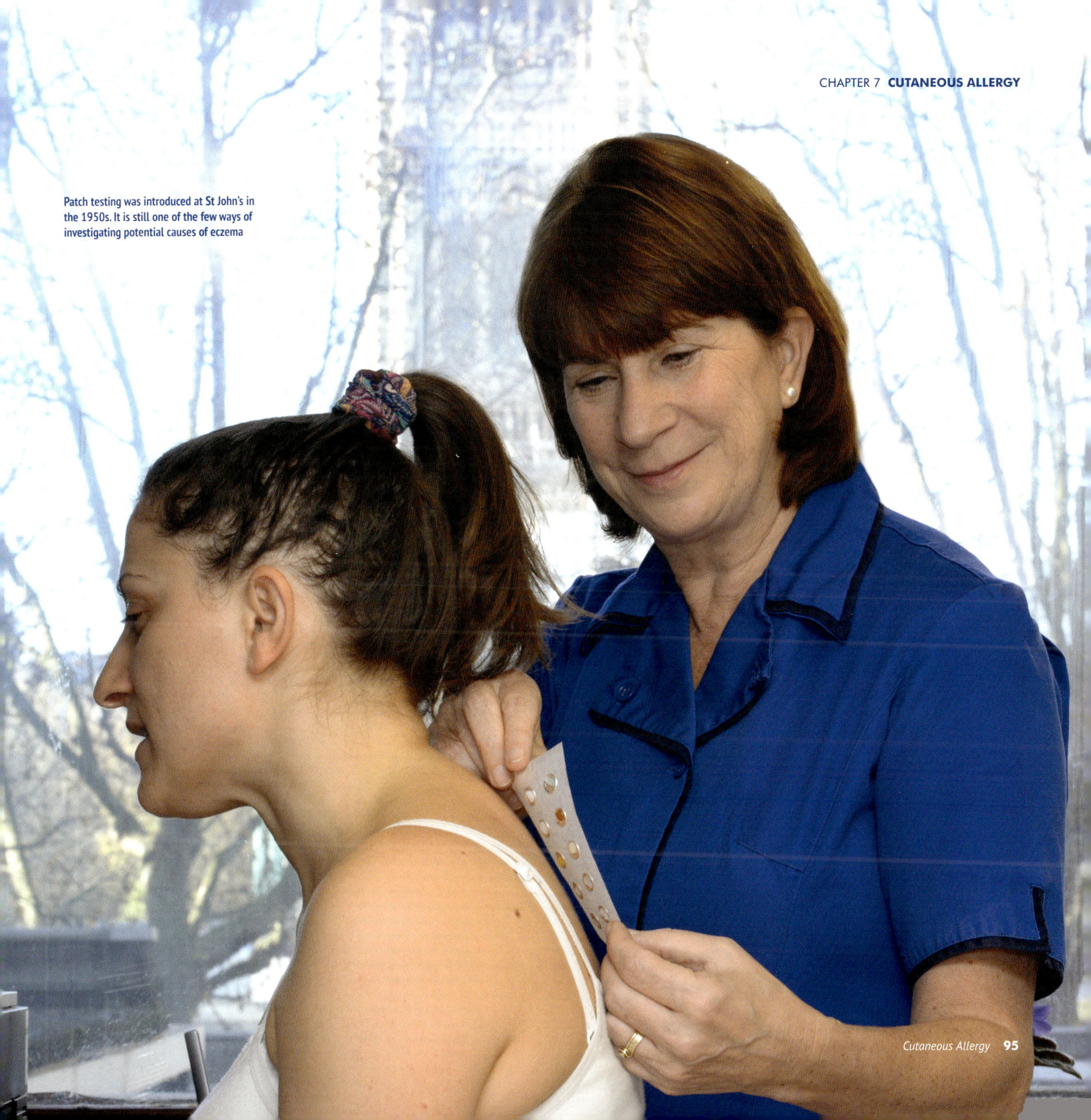

of the international journal *Contact Dermatitis*.

The basic methodology of patch testing that he introduced is largely unchanged, although the quality and range of the allergens has improved and standardised chambers are now used. Calnan was joined in the mid-1960s by **Etain Cronin**, an internationally recognised expert at patch testing who published a highly regarded book, *Contact Dermatitis*, in 1980.

Etain Cronin

Commercially available allergens prepared in syringes

Allergens are stored refrigerated

Patch test results are recorded in a standard format

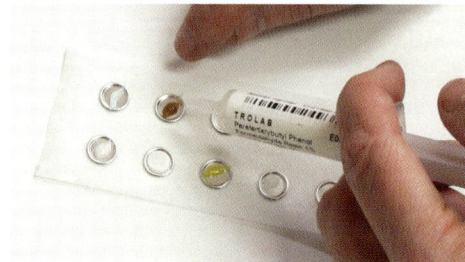
Finn Chambers being filled. Proper dosing of the chambers is important

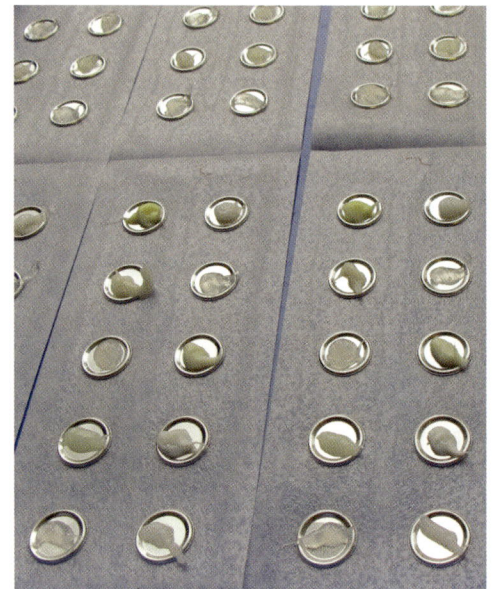
Filled Finn Cambers

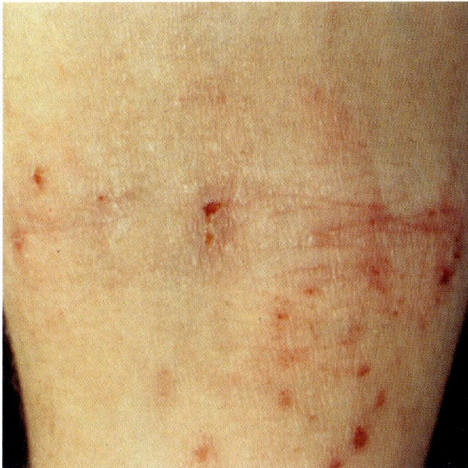

Atopic eczema, the most common form of eczema, mostly affects children

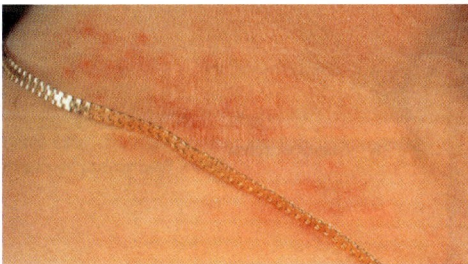

Allergic contact dermatitis caused by nickel in jewellery

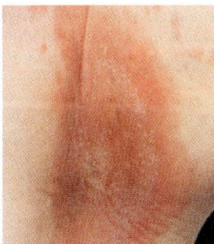

Irritant contact dermatitis

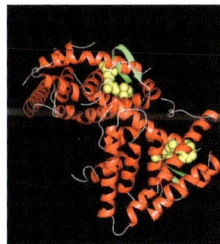

Alitretinoin

Types of eczema

There are three main types of dermatitis (or eczema):

1 Endogenous eczema – caused by genetic predisposition which results in the skin condition emerging regardless of the environment to which the individual is exposed. "Even if someone is confined to the stocks on an iceberg in the middle of the ocean the eczema will still develop," said Dr White.

2 Allergic contact dermatitis – an allergic reaction to a specific substance such as nickel in earrings – the typical Type 4 hypersensitivity reaction

3 Irritant contact dermatitis – caused by exposure to one or more substances with irritant potential and which produce inflammation by direct chemical or physical damage to the skin. Often there are repeated exposures, each causing minor changes to the skin until a threshold is breached and clinical signs of inflammation appear.

Often cases involve a combination of two or all three of the above types.

In the past, important causes of contact dermatitis seen in the clinic were occupational – the result of exposure to chemicals and substances used in industry. In the early 1970s, **Richard Rycroft**, joined St John's. He was employed by the Employment Medical Advisory Service of the Health and Safety Executive, and he developed the internationally recognised occupational dermatology service.

In the ensuing decades, as safety standards in industry rose and factories in London and across the country closed, the patients seen at St John's changed. The number of patients with problems caused by occupational exposure declined while the number with reactions to consumer products rose.

"We used to see a lot of occupational skin disease.

But the way people work has changed, thanks to Health and Safety regulations brought in during the 1970s and 1980s. They have transformed working practices and the exposures have changed enormously," said Dr White.

Richard Rycroft

Prevention is the goal but once the *dermatitis* is established, treatment is required. Treatments for *eczema* are based, as they long have been, around moisturisers and topical steroids for symptomatic relief. In severe cases of *eczema*, when there is a strong endogenous component, systemic immunosuppressive agents such as ciclosporin and azathioprine are used. More recently alitretinoin, a vitamin A derivative, has become available for the treatment of *hyperkeratotic hand and foot eczema*, where the skin becomes thick and fissured.

Mechanism of action of ciclosporin

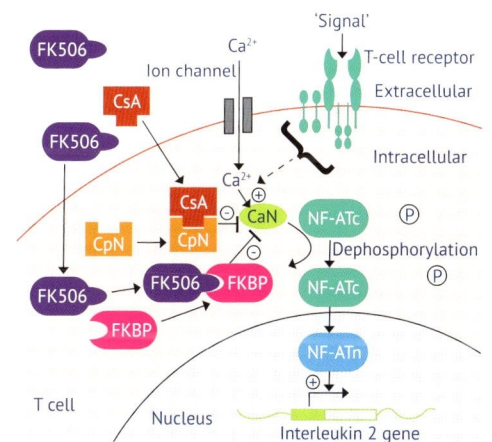

Mechanism of action of ciclosporin – a treatment for severe cases of eczema which suppresses the immune system

Occupational allergies

Today, a significant proportion of the patients seen at St John's who are suffering from occupational contact dermatitis work in the health service. That may sound odd as hospitals and clinics are among the cleanest environments. But repeated hand washing and wearing gloves, now required of all health workers in the battle against hospital infections, is an issue for people with an atopic tendency. Modern hand cleansers are milder than traditional tablet soap, but while they minimise the problem they cannot remove it.

Ian White   John McFadden   Jonathan White   Piu Banerjee

In the past latex gloves were a particular problem for health workers. When universal precautions were introduced over contact with patients in the 1980s in the wake of the HIV/Aids epidemic, hospitals began using cheap latex gloves from Asia and the Far East. These had not been properly treated to remove the proteins in the rubber which eluted out during wear causing allergic contact *urticaria* (Type 1 allergy) in large numbers of people.

The problem was solved when manufacturing standards were raised or gloves were sourced elsewhere and synthetic rubber gloves were introduced. Dr White said: "The problem has disappeared. I have not seen a genuine new case of latex protein allergy for several years."

Caterers also suffer with *contact dermatitis* as a result of exposure to fruit and vegetable juices. Chefs cutting up potatoes and peeling vegetables are often seen as patients of St John's.

Bricklayers, whose hands are frequently coated with wet cement, used to beat a constant path to the Institute complaining of rashes, rough skin and soreness. Cement is alkaline and thus an irritant, but in addition it contains a chemical, hexavalent chromium, which is a known allergen. Since 2005 the addition of ferrous sulfate to cement has eliminated exposure to hexavalent chromium in cement. Thanks in part to awareness of the problems it caused raised by St John's, the next generation of builders are protected from this devastating disease.

But management can be tricky. A worker laying floor tiles using epoxy resin-based cement complained of an allergic reaction on his hands despite wearing gloves. Doctors at St John's pointed out that if he was wearing gloves all day there would be more epoxy resin inside the gloves than out.

Dr White said: "The aim is to keep people at work and the treatment often consists of identifying the cause of their allergy and advising them on how to avoid exposure. In that way we cure people. That is rare in medicine."

Bricklayers suffered frequent rashes and sore skin until the composition of cement was changed in 2005

The clinic's global reputation means its dermatologists – there are currently four consultants in the department: **Ian White**, **John McFadden**, **Jonathan White** and **Piu Banerjee** – are in demand to give lectures in the UK and overseas and help promote cutaneous allergy and occupational dermatology services in developing countries. "In many countries where there is a wide manufacturing base and high prevalence of *occupational dermatitis* the patch testing service is still underdeveloped" said Dr McFadden.

Repeated handwashing (above) and use of detergents (below) are now required of health workers to prevent hospital infections and can cause problems in people with sensitive skin

Cosmetics

When ingredient labelling of cosmetics was introduced in 1993, fragrances were omitted – yet they are second only to nickel as a cause of allergic reactions

The ingredients of all cosmetics are listed on the label. That may seem a small matter to shout about – but it took a 15 year campaign to achieve and was only introduced in 2005. Even then fragrances were exempted.

"It transformed the outlook for allergy sufferers. Now they can look at the label and if they are allergic to, say, a formaldehyde releasing preservative, they can avoid it. It has revolutionised our ability to investigate and treat allergy," said Dr White.

The campaign began in the late 1980s and St John's played a prominent role from the start. Representatives of the industry claimed listing ingredients would confuse consumers. "'They don't need to know', was their view," said Dr White.

There were meetings with the Departments of Health and Trade and Industry and the EU Commission. Gradually opposition to labelling was beaten down. "I am not a laboratory-based researcher, I am someone who bangs on people's doors. If you bang on them long enough eventually they will open up and let you in," said Dr White.

That is what happened. Ingredient labelling of cosmetics was finally introduced following an EU ruling in 1993. But fragrances – the substances that give the products their smell – were exempted, because, it was claimed, they were too complicated to list. Confidentiality of formulations was also an issue. The fragrance manufacturers were a powerful lobby.

When the EU Directive requiring cosmetics to list their ingredients on the label came in, fragrances were excluded.

In 1999, the issue was re-examined by the *Scientific Committee on Cosmetics and Non-food products*. It said there were 26 important fragrance chemicals which consumers needed to be aware of and labelling was mandated by another EU ruling from March 2005.

Given there were around 3,000 fragrance substances in use, this should not have been a great problem for the cosmetics industry. But manufacturers protested. They demanded a review claiming some of the 26 named chemicals were not important as the level of exposure in the population was low.

In response the EU commissioned Dr White to conduct the review. The outcome was not what the industry had hoped. After a three year study, including public hearings, the review committee published an exhaustive 334 page report which was adopted in June 2012. It confirmed that the original 26 chemicals named in the first report remained suspect. In addition it identified further suspect chemicals it said should be listed, bringing the total to 83.

Three substances should be banned, it said: atranol and chloratranol, constituents of tree and oak moss, used in perfumes to provide "woody notes" but which are "extreme allergens"; and hydroxyisohexyl 3-cyclohexene carboxaldehyde (HICC), a synthetic substance widely used in skin care products to provide a floral aroma for more than a decade. An estimated 1.5 per cent of the population of Europe has become allergic to HICC as a result of this exposure.

A further 13 chemicals should be restricted including citral, found in lemon and tangerine oil, coumarin, found in spicy tonka beans, and isoeugenol, a component of rose oil.

The report, which estimated 16 per cent of patients with *eczema* were "sensitised to fragrance ingredients", triggered a war of words between the

Oak moss (above) and Tree moss (below): used in perfumes to provide woody notes but both are extreme allergens

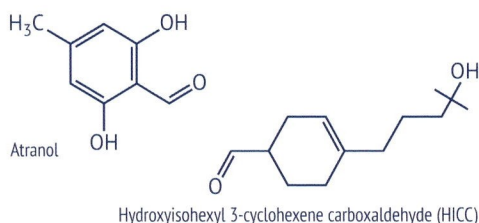

Hydroxyisohexyl 3-cyclohexene carboxaldehyde (HICC)

Lemon Myrtle

Tangerine Oil

perfume houses behind some of the biggest cosmetics and the dermatologists committed to protecting their patients. News reports appeared warning that consumers could be left without their favourite scent because of meddling EU bureaucrats. "It would be the end of beautiful perfumes if we could not use these ingredients," Françoise Montenay, the non-executive chairman of Chanel, told Reuters.

The protests highlighted oak moss, which manufacturers pointed out had been used as a constituent of perfume brands such as Chanel for more than 90 years.

Dr White responded: "This is not a trivial problem. After nickel, fragrances are the most important cause of contact allergy. Most things applied to the skin contain fragrances of one sort or another: deodorants, hand creams, body sprays. When susceptible people put these things on their skin they get *eczema*."

The industry claimed the report was an attack on some of Europe's most famous fashion houses. But Dr White pointed out that it was possible to extract the harmful chemicals without affecting the smell of the perfume. "Oak moss contains chemicals which are extreme allergens. The manufacturers know this perfectly well. They have funded research to reduce them – they can extract these ingredients so the other constituents of the moss can still be used," he said.

Since 2005, the 26 chemicals named in the first review have been listed on labels. EU member states are expected to ratify a new regulation banning the three named substances and extending the labelling requirement to the chemicals named in the second review.

"It has been a 25 year battle but we are nearly there," said Dr White.

Cosmetics again

1.	Nickel sulfate	5%	
2.	Disperse Yellow 3	1%	
3.	Colophonium	20%	
4.	2-Bromo-2-nitropropane-1,3-diol	0.5%	
5.	p-Phenylenediamine	1%	
6.	MBT	2%	
7.	Formaldehyde	2%	
8.	Potassium dichromate	0.5%	
9.	Lanolin alcohol	30%	
10.	Fragrance Mix II	14%	
11.	Paraben mix	1%	
12.	Neomycin	20%	
13.	Cobalt chloride	1%	
14.	Quaternium - 15	1%	
15.	p-Chloro-m-cresol	1%	
16.	Thiuram mix	1%	
17.	Mercapto mix	1%	
18.	Fragrance mix I	8%	
19.	IPPD	0.1%	
20.	Sesquiterpene lactone mix	0.1%	
21.	Clioquinol	5%	
22.	PTBP resin	1%	
23.	MCI/MI	0.02%	
24.	Caine mix	10.0%	
25.	Myroxylon pereirae (balsam of Peru)	25%	
26.	Imidazolidinyl urea	2%	
27.	Tixocortol pivalate	0.1%	
28.	Cetearyl alcohol	20%	
29.	Phenoxyethanol	1%	
30.	Dermovate cream		
31.	Betnovate cream		
32.	Budesonide	0.1%	
33.	Diazolidinyl urea	2%	
34.	Methyldibromo glutaronitrile	0.3%	
35.	Epoxy Resin	1%	
36.	Sodium Metabisulfite	1%	
37.	Methylisothiazolinone	0.2%	
38.	Sorbic acid	2%	
39.	Octylisothiazolinone	0.1%	
40.	Benzisothiazolinone	0.05%	
41.			
42.			

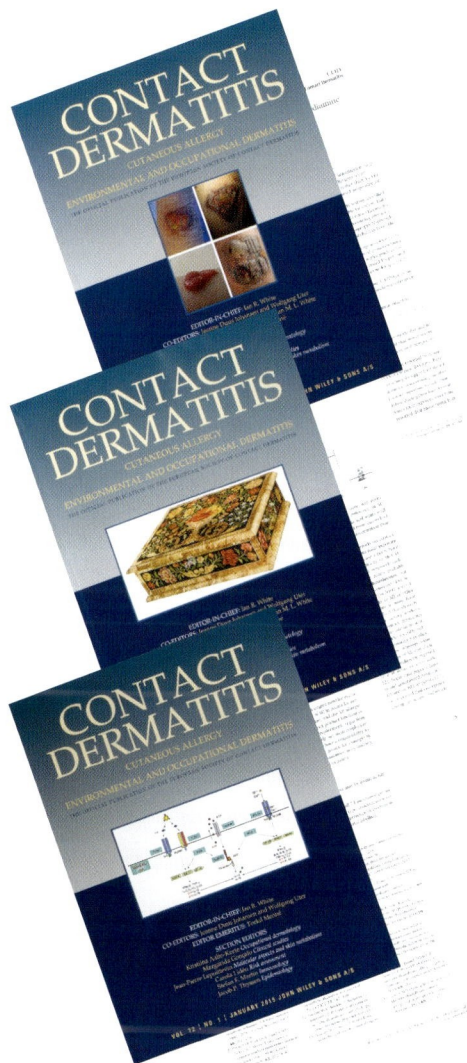

The journal Contact Dermatitis started in 1975 by Charles Calnan remains the most important publication relevant to the specialty. It is now also the official publication of the European Society of Contact Dermatitis

The baseline series of contact allergens used at St. John's is regularly updated

One in ten patients tested at St John's is allergic to the preservative methylisothiazolinone used in cometics.

Methylisothiazolinone

As one problem is resolved, another raises its head. Methylisothiazolinone (MI) is a preservative that has increasingly been used in cosmetics over the last decade. A risk assessment in 2003 concluded it was safe in both leave-on and rinse-off products.

However, in 2011, dermatologists at St John's started seeing patients who were allergic to MI and by 2013 it had become an epidemic, according to Dr White. "One in ten of our patch tested patients are now allergic to it," he said.

The EU were, once again, slow to act. Despite being alerted to the problem by St John's in early 2012, the EU authorities at first ignored it and then dismissed it as of low priority. When reports started appearing in the media they asked the *Scientific Committee on Consumer Safety*, chaired by Dr White, to review it.

In December 2013, the committee concluded that MI should be prohibited in leave-on cosmetic products, including wet wipes, and restricted to 15 parts per million (ppm) in rinse-off products.

At the same time, the industry trade association called on manufacturers to cease using MI in leave-on products, including wet wipes. But it made no recommendation about rinse-off products.

Dr White said: "The MI problem will, belatedly, be resolved in Europe. But will the lessons be learned? In a few years, no doubt, we will experience another catastrophe. The cosmetics industry must have faith in the clinical data generated and given freely by the dermatological community. Safety cannot continue to be a competition."

A case of nickel allergy (above) and (below) 5p nickel coins introduced in 2013. Studies have shown the nickel released from the coins is seven times higher than the legal limit

5p Nickel coins

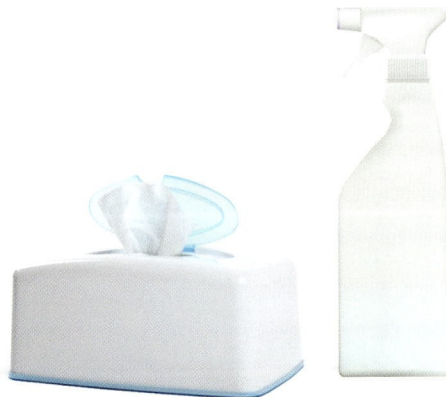

Millions of people are sensitive to chemicals in cosmetics and household products and are liable to develop rashes, weals or other skin reactions from contact with them

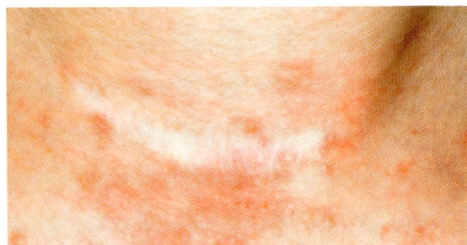

Nickel

Nickel is a common cause of allergy affecting around one in ten people. It is acquired from exposure to the metal, often as a result of contact with nickel-containing jewellery, such as ear studs. It is therefore more common in women, affecting around 17 per cent.

Denmark was the first country to restrict exposure to nickel in the 1980s. A decade later in 1994, the restriction was extended across Europe by the *EU Nickel Directive*. This set a limit on the amount that could be released onto the skin of 0.5 micrograms per sq cm, per week.

However, the nickel in coins remains an uncontrolled risk, according to experts at St John's who have campaigned to have it removed. In April 2013, the UK Government introduced new 5p and 10p coins made of nickel-plated steel which it claimed would save the Treasury £7 million a year.

Studies in Sweden have shown that nickel released from the new UK coins was seven times higher than the legal limit for other nickel-containing products. The Swedes carried out a risk assessment and concluded the coins were not safe for consumers because of the risk they might cause *contact dermatitis*. Nickel coins were rejected in Sweden.

In the UK, a risk assessment concluded the coins had no effect on health. But enquiries by St John's revealed that this was based on the observation that the coins were marketed in other countries and there had been no complaints. The Royal Mint had not undertaken any formal risk assessment.

In an editorial in *Contact Dermatitis* in 2012, Dr White and colleagues wrote: "Nickel exposure from coins could be the straw that broke the camel's back in many nickel-allergic individuals with hand eczema. It is time to rethink the use of nickel in coins."

Hair dye

After nickel, hair dye is one of the most common and potent allergens – with widespread population exposure. Reactions range from mild irritation of the scalp to severe dermatitis, redness, swelling and a weeping scalp.

In the worst cases the face may swell causing difficulty breathing. In May 2000, a 38 year old mother of three, **Narinder Devi**, collapsed and died after using hair dye at her home in Edgbaston, Birmingham.

A year later scientists at the University of California published research suggesting women who dyed their hair for more than 15 years doubled their risk of *bladder cancer*.

The European Commission set up a working party in response to growing concerns about hair dyes. It critically reviewed the safety of more than 100 hair dyeing chemicals used by industry. But it warned that individuals were still at risk of an allergic reaction to many of the dyes.

Dr White said: "The problem is that many hair dyes are extreme or potent allergens. You cannot ban them because of the social need that has developed. The industry is trying to develop alternatives and one new one is already on the market. Those that come up with safer alternatives will have a competitive advantage."

Dr McFadden, author of a doctoral thesis and a number of papers on hair dye allergy, said: "One of the difficult aspects has been understanding the nature and mechanisms of sensitisation. Now that these aspects are beginning to be better understood, there is a real prospect of reducing hair dye allergy rates."

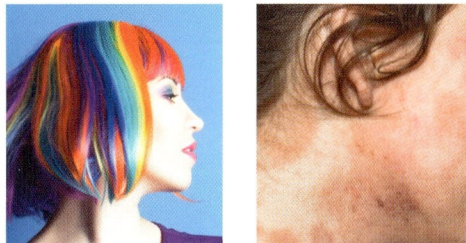

Hair dyes are potent allergens and can cause reactions ranging from mild irritation to severe dermatitis

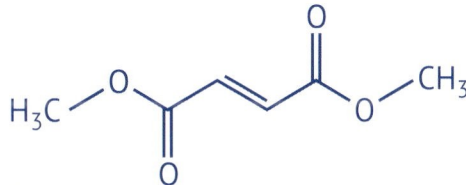

Dimethyl fumarate

A toxic fungicide used in leather sofas caused an outbreak of "furniture-related dermatitis" in 2006-8

Sofas

From 2006-8, there was an outbreak of furniture-related dermatitis in the UK and in some neighbouring countries including France and Finland. People began turning up at St John's with severe, red, swollen rashes on their back, buttocks and the backs of their legs. In some cases the rash went septic and the patient had to be hospitalised. Over 5,000 people were affected.

Investigation revealed that all patients had recently bought leather couches which were imported from China. The condition came to be know as *toxic sofa dermatitis*.

The cause was a fungicide – dimethyl fumarate – which was used to prevent the growth of mould. It was packaged in small sachets, similar to silica gel sachets used to remove moisture, which were stapled to the wooden frame or directly under the leather covering.

Transporting sofas across the world and through different climates leads to moisture build up and the growth of mould and the use of dimethyl fumarate was a way of counteracting this problem.

What the manufacturers had not realised is that the chemical is a potent allergen which permeates the leather goods as it evaporates. Allergic individuals who sat on the sofas developed reactions, even when they were clothed. Many filed lawsuits.

Dimethyl fumarate has since been banned in Europe, and the problem has disappeared. "We now see only the occasional case," said Dr White. But for a few years sofa dermatitis added an extra dimension to warnings about the health hazards of spending too much time on the couch.

A 34-year old non-atopic physiotherapist presented with a 6-month history of hand eczema, which developed several weeks after the birth of her first child. Examination showed diffuse eczematous changes over the palmar aspect of her hands; her skin elsewhere was not affected.

Diagnostic patch test investigations revealed contact allergy to the preservatives methylisothiazolinone, octylisothiazolinone and also to the fragrance substances citral, oxidised limonene and hydroxyisohexyl 3-cyclohexene carboxaldehyde. As in Europe there is now ingredient labelling of cosmetic (skincare) products and household detergents, it was possible to identify her current exposure to methylisothiazolinone in wet wipes she was using on her new baby. Additionally, she had current exposures to citral and limonene in several of the cleaning products she was using at home. Avoidance of these allergens resulted in resolution of her *hand eczema*.

Three months after returning to work, she attended with an *acute facial eczema* that occurred the day after returning home from a short break out of the country. Whilst away, her husband had painted the living room and bedroom of their flat. He had used a well-known brand of paint; there was no declaration of content on the paint container, no warnings or other relevant information.

Paints may contain isothiazolinone preservatives although manufactures are not obliged to reveal this as methylisothiazolinone is not classified as an

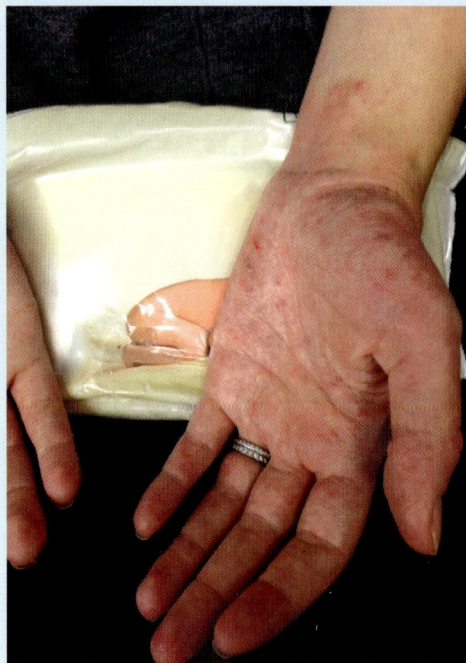

Allergic contact dermatitis caused by the preservative in a wet wipe product for babies

allergen under existing legislation (Classification for Labelling and Packaging) covering such products and, therefore, may not appear on product safety data sheets. We were able to advise that any isothiazolinones would dissipate over a week if the rooms were well-ventilated. Subsequent chemical analysis confirmed the presence of both methylisothiazolinone and octylisothiazolinone in the paint.

Ingredient labelling of cosmetic and household products has transformed the management of patients with *contact allergy*. Quality of life has

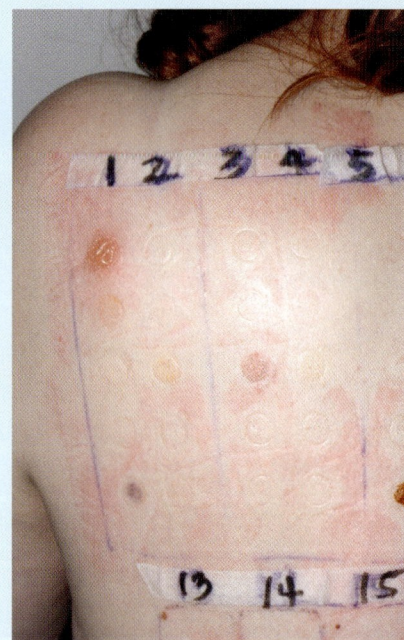

dramatically improved for such patients, a fact that is often not appreciated for such a simple intervention. The goal now is to achieve full ingredient listing for all types of products that may be encountered at home and at work.

*"The cosmetics industry must have faith in
the clinical data generated and given freely
by the dermatological community.
Safety cannot continue to be a competition."*

THE NURSE'S ROLE

An out-patient service

One of the biggest changes in St John's 150 year history has occurred within the last decade – the closure of its in-patient wards. Instead of admitting patients to hospital for six to eight weeks at a time – a frequent occurrence in the past – today the department manages the vast majority as outpatients, thanks to advances in drug treatments and phototherapy.

In turn this has transformed the role from primarily ward based healthcare workers to the highly skilled specialised nurses of today. These specialised nurses may manage cases, administer day treatment or phototherapy, prescribe medicines, carry out surgery, and look after patients with highly complex needs who are living at home. They set national standards and guidelines and have conducted training courses across the globe.

Nowhere is the transformation in the way patients are cared for – and the role of the nurses caring for them – clearer than in the treatment of inflammatory skin diseases such as *psoriasis*, *eczema* and blistering conditions. Patients with severe

Edward Ward at St Thomas' in the 1950s

psoriasis comprised most of the in-patient population in the past.

St John's had two 28 bedded wards at one point. Patients could be admitted for many weeks and receive daily topical treatments to control their skin condition.

Today, patients are still treated with lotions, creams and ointments in much the same way as in past decades but in a day centre rather than a ward. Applying lotions to the skin is a laborious, time consuming process but can provide remission. Care is provided by dermatologically trained Registered Nurses and Nursing Assistants, who all play crucial roles in the out-patient setting.

The last in-patient ward was closed in 2005. Today, the **Dermatology Day Centre** provides the same treatment with one difference – at night the patients go home. Some come three times a week and spend two to three hours having topical treatments and complicated wound dressings applied by the skilled nurses, most of whom have undertaken specialist training on caring for severe skin conditions. Occasionally, the patients worst

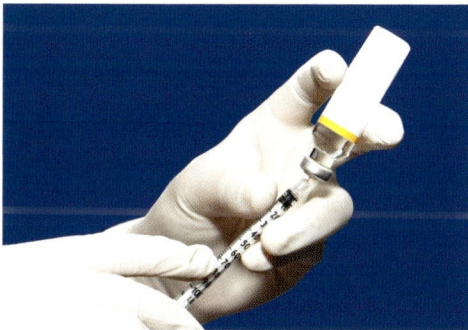

Biologic treatments are administered by injection

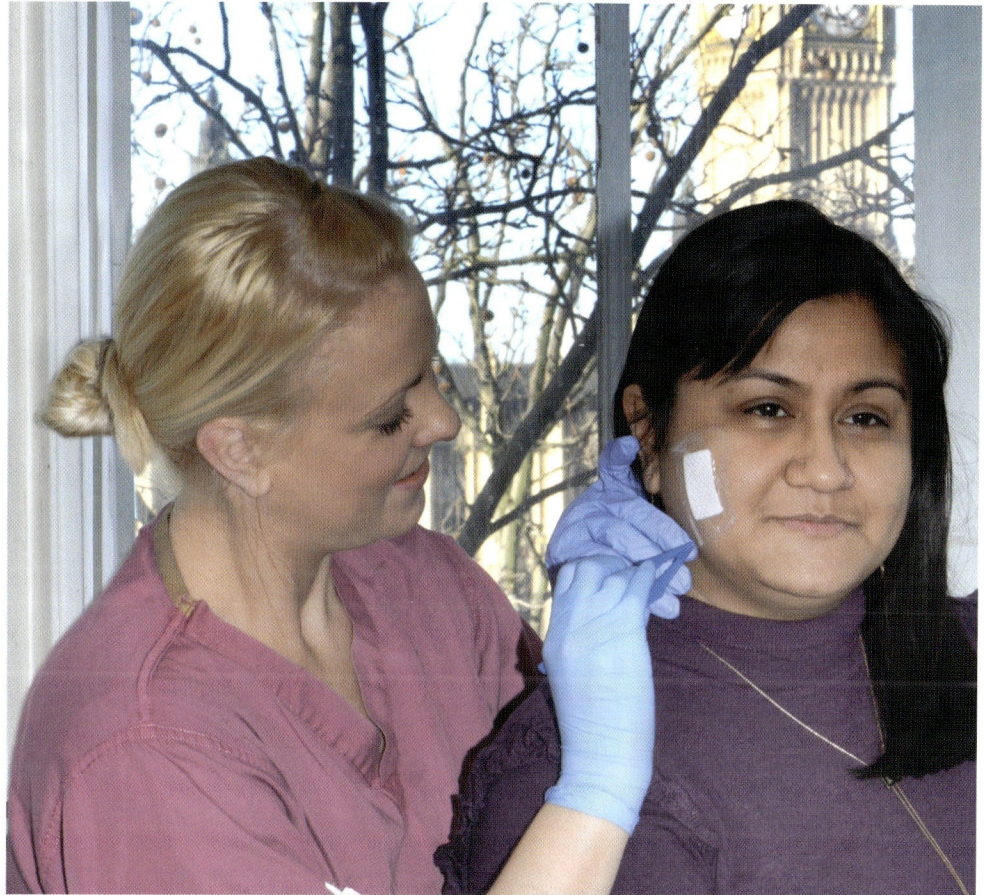

Nurse led skin surgery and wound care: some patients come three times a week for treatment but no longer need to be admitted as in-patients

affected will spend a week or two in the unit, staying in hospital accommodation if they live far away. But the real transformation in the treatment of *psoriasis* and some skin blistering conditions has been achieved through the introduction of the new biologic drugs. This can be seen in the figures. In 2003-4 there were over 120 in-patient admissions for *psoriasis*. Three years later there were fewer than 10. The impact on patients has been dramatic. But it presented new challenges for nurses.

Karina Jackson, nurse consultant and clinical lead for the day centre, said: "We are keeping *psoriasis* patients out of hospital by using highly effective but potentially dangerous drugs. But finding the right therapy can take months. Some people fail on one drug and need to try another. They start with standard therapy – *ciclosporin and methotrexate* – and if these are not helpful, then may move on to the biologics. Much of our work now is running drug initiation and monitoring clinics, supporting and coordinating patient care. We take at least 50 calls a day from patients who need advice about their treatment or are worried about side effects or concerned about their progress."

The Dermatology Day Centre is open seven days a week and the nursing team treat patients with a range of inflammatory or blistering skin conditions, some requiring woundcare. Those worst affected are still admitted as in-patients, if they are acutely unwell. But today they will be treated on an acute ward in the Trust, visited by clinical nurse specialists from St John's who will develop their skin treatment plan alongside other specialists, prescribe drugs such as steroids for *eczema*, and ensure they receive the best multidisciplinary care. The specialist nurses who do this also train other hospital nurses on caring for people with a skin condition.

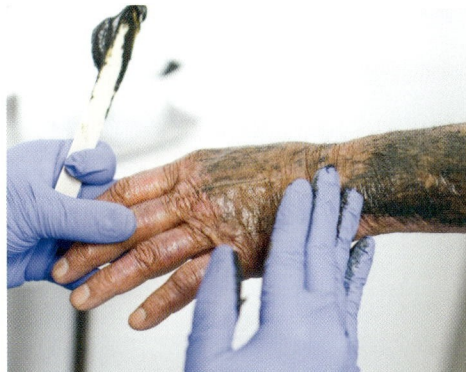

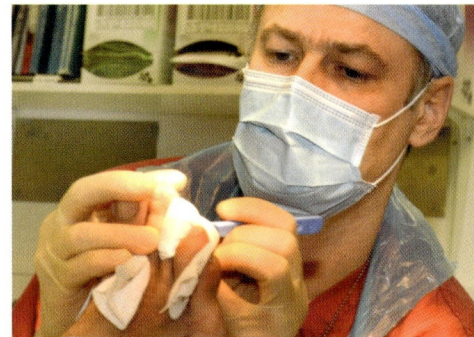

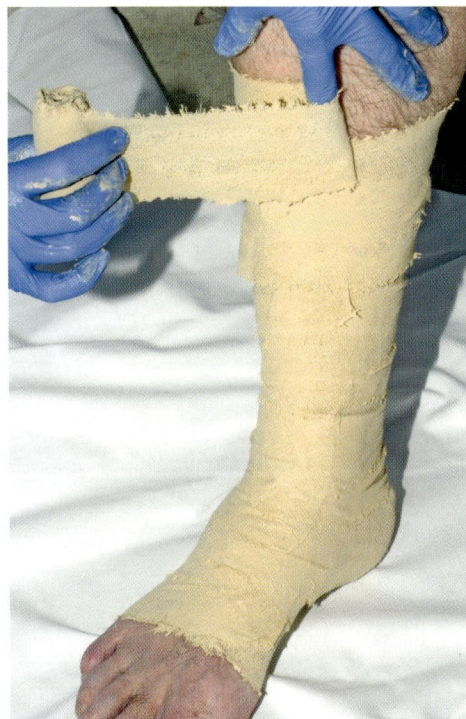

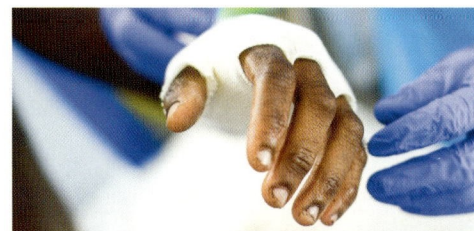

Karina Jackson

Longstanding treatments such as coal tar ointment and paste bandages are still used in the Dermatology Day Centre with good effect

The six specialties

Records show that the first matron of St John's – Fanny Edwards – was appointed in 1869. Thousands have followed in her footsteps and today the Institute has 63 nurses (including a nurse consultant, three matrons and a head of nursing) of whom 25 are clinical nurse specialists. They are divided between six specialties: medical dermatology, skin cancer, cutaneous allergy, surgery and laser treatment, photodermatology and paediatrics. They also support two nationally-commissioned services for rare but severe conditions: *Epidermolysis Bullosa and Xeroderma Pigmentosa.*

While the nurse specialists in medical dermatology treat mainly patients with severe *eczema*, *psoriasis* and blistering conditions, in skin cancer they have taken on some of the tasks formerly performed by doctors .

The clinical nurse specialist for minor surgical procedures at St John's operates on patients with suspicious moles or other lesions, and helps to train junior doctors in biopsy technique. Biopsies are samples of tissue taken for examination in the laboratory.

Skin cancer screening clinics at St John's are run on the one-stop-shop principle so patients with a suspect skin lesion do not have to make multiple appointments.

Patients who come to the skin cancer screening clinic are assessed by a dermatologist or a skin cancer clinical nurse specialist first. If the patient has a suspicious lesion it can be biopsied or removed on the same day.

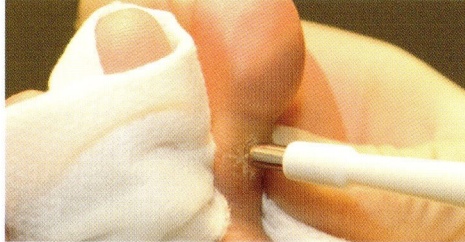

There are 25 Clinical Nurse Specialists at St John's

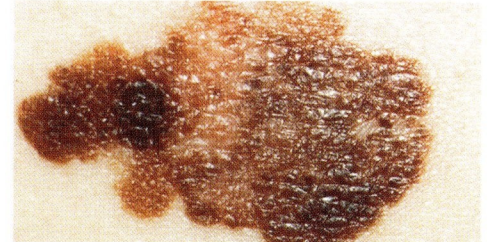

Nurse specialists operate on patients with suspicious moles

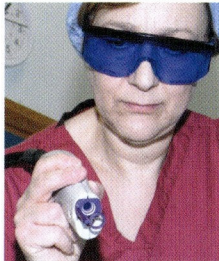

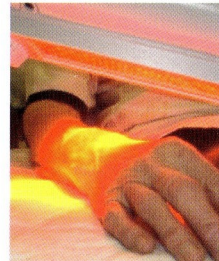

Nurses operate lasers for removal of birthmarks and port wine stains

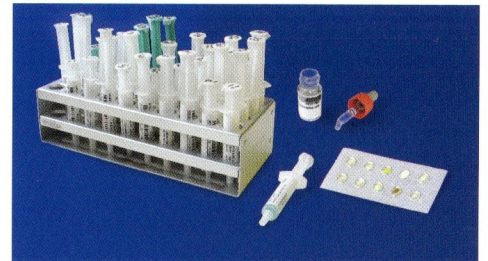

Nurses administer diagnostic tests for allergies

Nurses deliver phototherapy for psoriasis

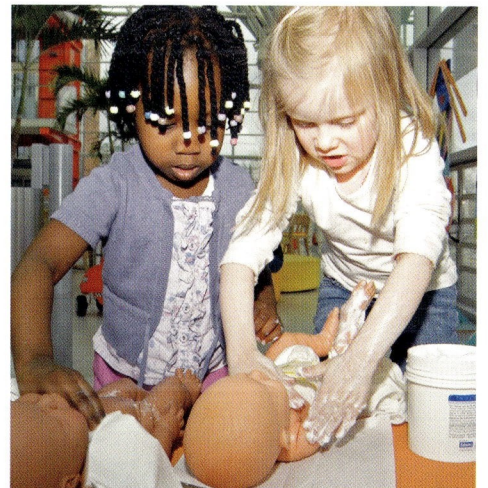

Nurses support families of children with EB

In the case of patients with disorders such as *Xeroderma Pigmentosum* and *Epidermolysis Bullosa* – both conditions that are extremely challenging to manage, especially in children - clinical nurse specialists will travel to the patients' home to give advice on clothing, dressing blisters, feeding and how to protect them from the sun and other sources of ultra violet light, as appropriate. They also advise teachers on how to support affected pupils. In the rare cases when the condition deteriorates and patients are admitted to hospital, they provide care.

Nurse specialists operate lasers for the removal of birthmarks and port wine stains. They deliver phototherapy for the treatment of *psoriasis* and other conditions. In paediatrics, nurses face an additional challenge - supporting the whole family. Working alongside the clinical nurses are a team of research nurses who play a key role in recruiting patients to research studies and clinical trials, which leads to the development of new treatments for skin disease.

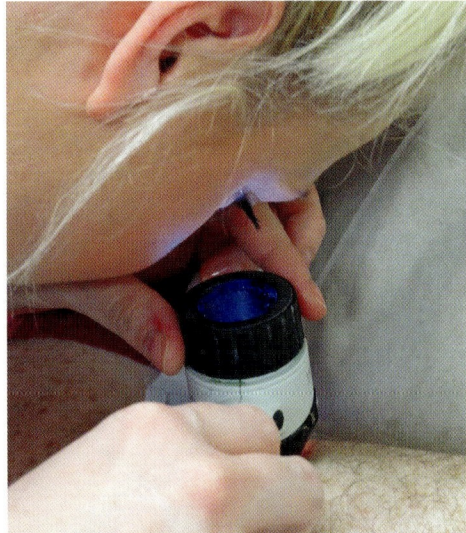
Nurses screen patients for skin cancer

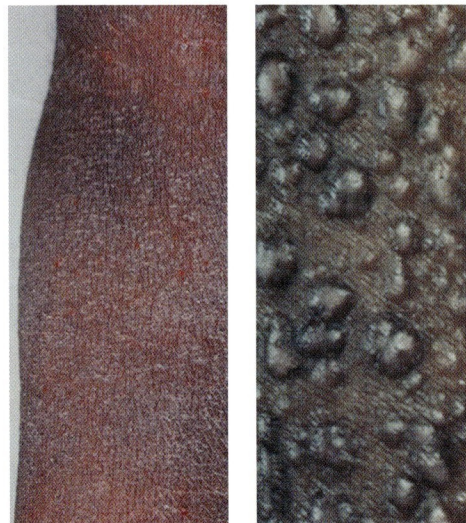
Nurses support families of children with EB

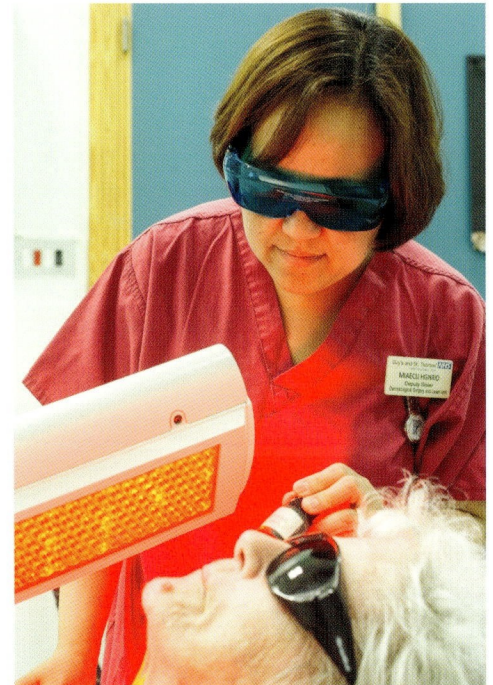
Atopic eczema (left) and nodular prurigo (right): today St John's has 63 nurses

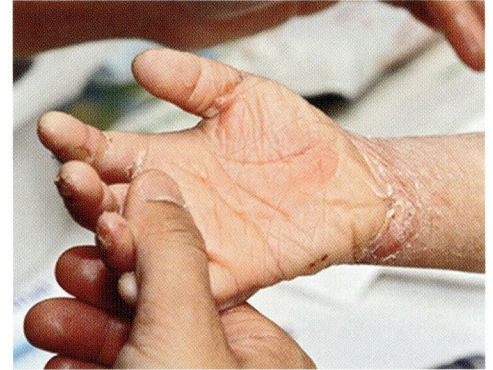
Nurse-led photo dynamic therapy (PDT) – a treatment for some skin cancers'

A nurse administering iontophoresis treatment (a weak electric current) to a patient with hyperhidrosis (excessive sweating). The nurse's role has been transformed from ward-based healthcare to highly skilled specialised work.

Maija Hansen

Maija Hansen, deputy head of nursing, said: "In paediatrics, nurses support children and their parents and teach them how to use the medicines. They must make sure the child understands what they can do for themselves and that they feel comfortable doing so and at the same time empower their parents to help."

A major growth area in the nursing workload has been in the use of extra corporeal photopheresis (ECP) for treating *cutaneous lymphoma* and *graft vs host disease* (a serious complication that can follow a bone marrow or stem cell transplant). This procedure involves withdrawing blood from the patient after the patient has taken a medicine called Psoralen. This medicine photo-sensitises the

Severe skin conditions are extremely challenging to manage in children. Nurses travel to their homes to provide support to the whole family.

white blood cells and they are then exposed to UVA light within the ECP machine. The patient's blood is then re-infused back to the patient.

Ms Hansen, said: "There has been an increase in patients with *graft vs host disease* in the last six years following bone marrow transplants. We are now treating 125 patients a month who have two sessions each, lasting 2-4 hours per treatment."

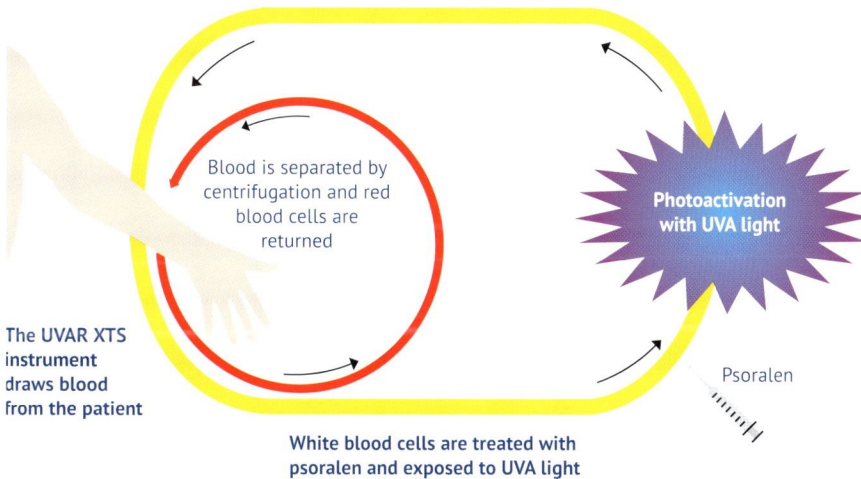

The UVAR XTS instrument draws blood from the patient

Blood is separated by centrifugation and red blood cells are returned

Photoactivation with UVA light

Psoralen

White blood cells are treated with psoralen and exposed to UVA light

A big growth area has been in extra corporeal photopheresis (ECP): a treatment which involves withdrawing the blood from a patient who has been treated with a drug, psoralen, then exposing the blood to UV light to trigger a response before re-infusing it into the body.

A nurse delivering ECP: St John's is treating 125 patients with ECP a month

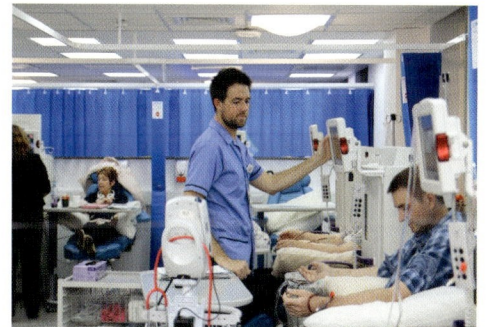

The ECP suite: each patient has two sessions of treatment lasting 2-4 hours

From lotions to potent skin creams

There has been a big change in the skin creams and topical treatments used in recent decades. The St John's pharmacy once featured hundreds of items, including *hamamelis* (witch hazel) used to produce a soothing ointment, oil of bergamot, the main ingredient of eau de cologne which was used to mask unpleasant smells and *hydrgyrum* (mercury) used in ointments, now known to be toxic. All these have been superseded today.

Some concoctions were specially made up for a single patient, to a recipe their doctor felt would be most appropriate. Small batches of medication with a short shelf life proved expensive and made achieving quality standards challenging. In recent times the British Association of Dermatologists has dramatically narrowed the list of approved treatments. Topical steroids and emollients – moisturisers that prevent water loss – are the mainstay today.

Skin conditions can be disfiguring and there is high demand for help with cosmetic camouflage to disguise the effects. Patients are assisted to select the right products, find the right mixture for their skin tone and are taught to apply them. For those with *alopecia* (hair loss) there is a hair clinic where they are helped to choose wigs.

There has been a big change in skin creams. Ingredients such as mercury (left), now known to be toxic, and Witch Hazel (right) have been superseded.

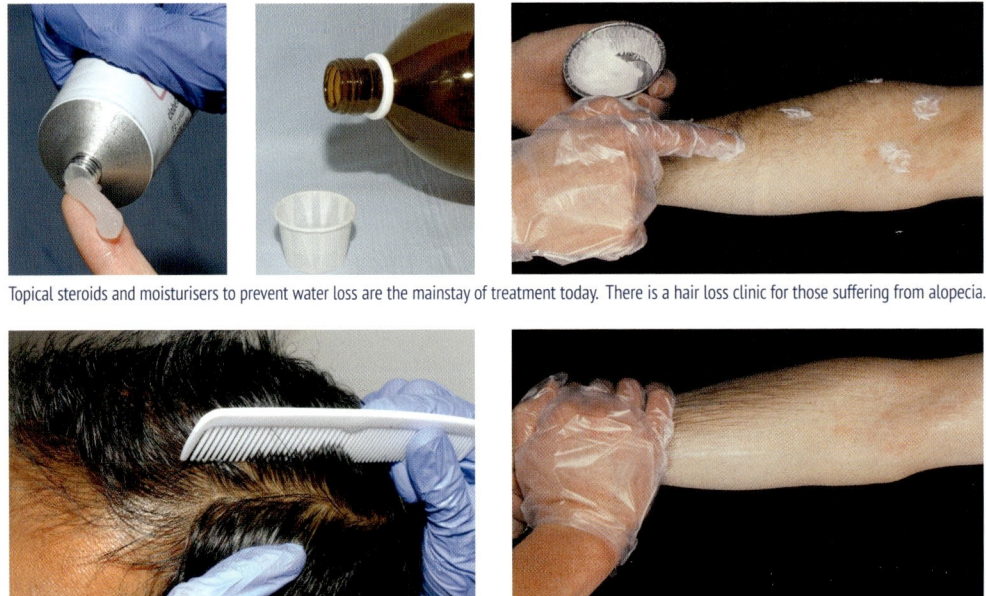

Topical steroids and moisturisers to prevent water loss are the mainstay of treatment today. There is a hair loss clinic for those suffering from alopecia.

The psychology of skin disease

Four-year-old Jaiden from Chelmsford started losing her hair 18 months ago. Her mum Sarah said: "She had no hair at all at one point. The GP wasn't sure what it was and we were eventually referred to St John's. Jaiden had a biopsy taken and was diagnosed with alopecia areata in March this year.

"The condition is normally caused by stress, but we're not sure what set it off. Her head is now covered in hair thanks to the treatment which involved a special type of shampoo that is only available through the clinic. She's starting school in September so it's brilliant that her hair has come back in time, as some of her friends had started to say things about her lack of hair.

"The children's hair loss clinic is brilliant. I don't know what we would have done if we hadn't been referred to it, as no one seemed to know what was causing her hair loss or how we could stop it."

The psychological and social impact of a disease that affects a patient's appearance can be severe. Some suffer a catastrophic effect on their ability to function and lead a normal life.

Lynette Stone, former head of nursing at St. John's oversaw the move of in-patient wards from east London to St Thomas' in the 1990's and she worked hard to ensure that patients' psychological needs were addressed by doctors and nurses.

Today the need for psychological support has been formally recognised with the appointment of a clinical psychologist to medical dermatology (most recently in February 2014), who provides therapy to patients and helps staff better understand and support patients' psychological needs.

"In the past nurses would often see patient distress and did what they could to provide emotional support but there was limited access to expert help. Now having trained psychologists in the department helps us provide support more confidently and we can refer patients for therapy if necessary," said Karina Jackson.

St John's nursing team has also established a course for parents of children with eczema, the first of its kind in the country. Parents are taught about the disease and available treatments, how to recognise infections and what triggers outbreaks. Anecdotal results suggest parents are more confident, the quality of life of their children has improved and GP visits have reduced.
"We are hoping to run a UK wide clinical trial," Ms Jackson said.

Education and training

Lynette Stone, with co-authors **Stuart Robertson** and **Helen Lindfield**, published the first textbook on dermatological nursing entitled *"Colour Atlas of Nursing Procedures in Skin Disorders"* in 1989. She was a founder member of the British Dermatology Nursing Group, which fostered the development of specialist skills and there is an annual Stone Award to celebrate dermatology nurses of distinction.

St John's established a course for nurses which was recognised by the English National Board in the 1990s as the first dermatology course in the UK. Short courses were also set up and nurse visitors started coming from abroad. An annual phototherapy training course for nurses is long established, led by Sister **Trish Garibaldinos**.

In 2006, Karina Jackson started a new dermatology care course, which was accredited by Kings College London and is offered at degree and MSc level. Ten to 15 nurses and others, such as podiatrists, undertake the course each year, drawn from London, the south east and further afield.

St John's also runs a number of short courses including pharmacology and prescribing, long term conditions and dermatology, phototherapy, and biologics.

Research Nurses play a key role in implementing and managing a large portfolio of research studies and clinical trials within St John's Institute of Dermatology which support the further development of treatments for skin disease.

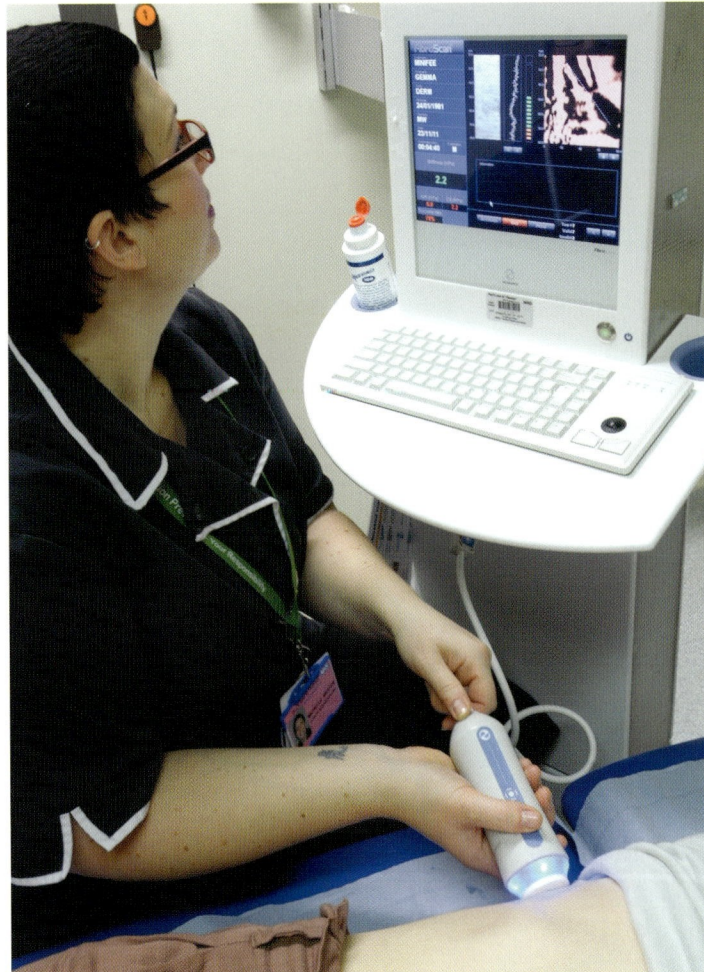

Lynette Stone: author of the first textbook in dermatological nursing (below)

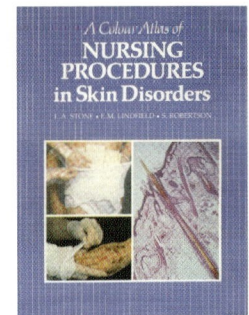

The first dermatology course for nurses in the UK was established at St John's in the 1990s. It now offers courses at degree and MSc level for 10-15 nurses, and others, each year.

All St John's nurses are encouraged to undertake specialist training courses to advance their knowledge and skills

St John's outpatient and specialist day care services moved into a state-of-the-art new home at Guy's Hospital in summer 2015. Part of the new Bermondsey Centre, dermatology services will be co-located with academic colleagues and research teams, as well as other specialties including allergy, lupus and rheumatology. They will also be located close to the new Cancer Centre and clinical genetics service, also at Guy's.

Welcome to
Bermondsey Centre
and
St. John's Institute of Dermatology
Reception

Patient
Check In

Scan Here

St JOHN'S
INSTITUTE
OF DERMATOLOGY

CELEBRATING

150 YEARS

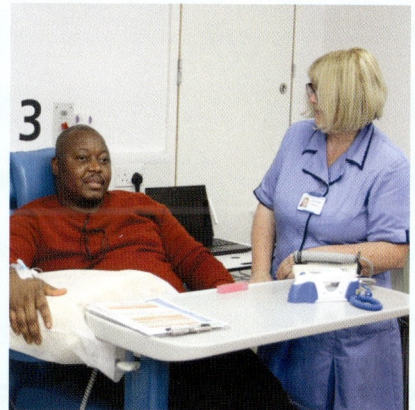

The Bermondsey Centre at Guy's has improved the experience of dermatology patients needing specialist treatment.

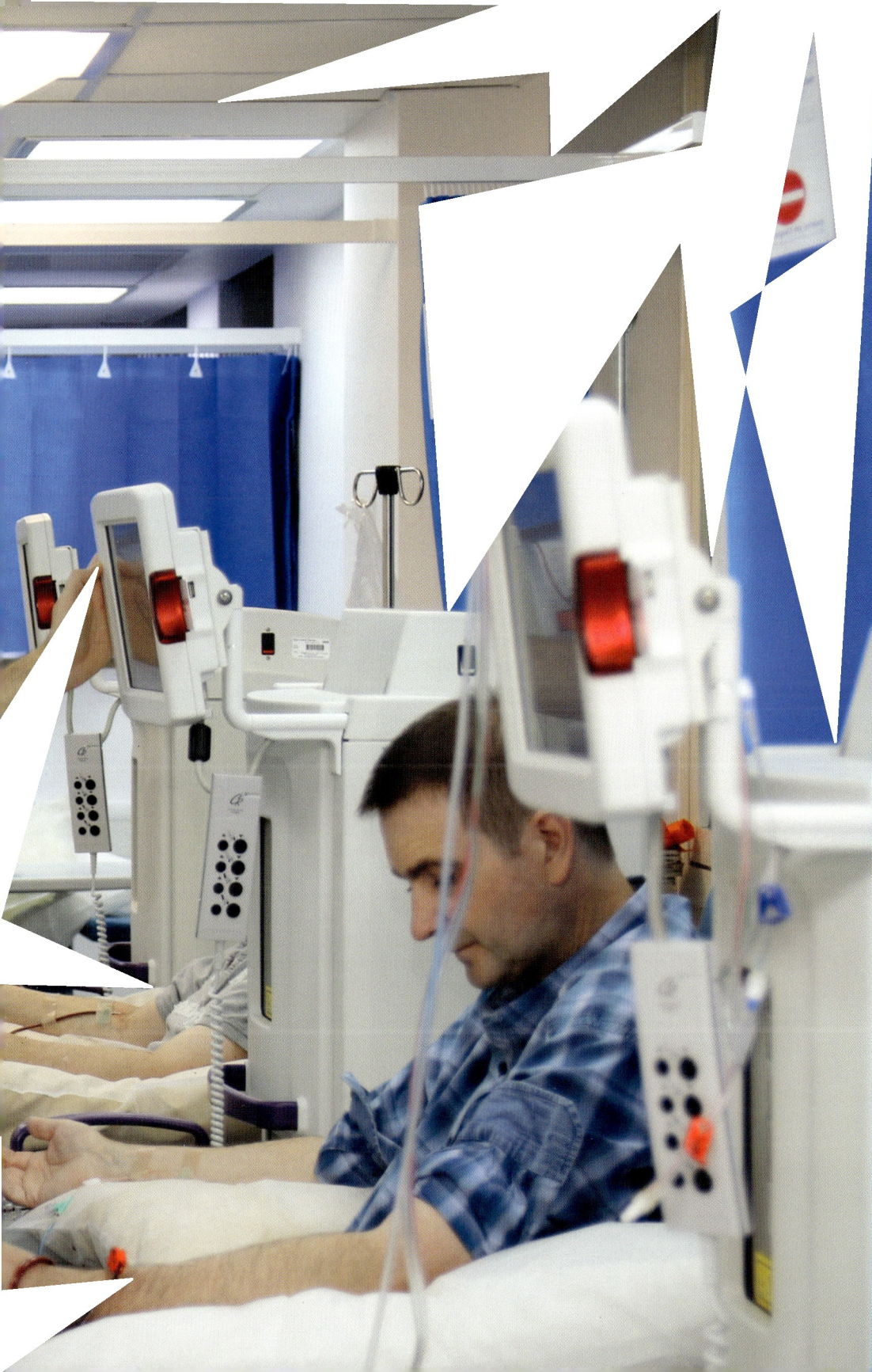

St JOHN'S INSTITUTE OF DERMATOLOGY STAFF

Clinical Director

Prof Sean Whittaker

Clinical Lead

Dr Richard Groves
Dr Raj Mallipeddi

Clinical Nurse Specialists

Mr Serhiy Aleksyeyenko
Ms Alison Baker
Mr Christopher Bloor
Ms Debra Brown
Ms Jane Clapham
Ms Victoria Critchley
Ms Helen Dennis
Ms Anette Downe
Ms Maricel Franco
Ms Trish Garibaldinos
Mr Ian Gosling
Ms Pauline Graham-King
Mr David Haigh
Ms Tanya Henshaw
Ms Jing Li
Ms Caroline McKenzie
Ms Erin Mewton
Ms Gemma Minifie
Ms Amanda Mogan
Ms Lucy Moorhead
Ms Catherine Morgans
Ms Gillian Ogden
Ms Elizabeth Pillay
Ms Katherine Radley
Ms Sukran Saglam
Ms Heather Sharp
Ms Bunmi Soji-Adeyemo

Ms Sally Turner
Ms Hui Zhang

Charge Nurse

Mr Idris Yussuf

Consultant Nurse

Ms Karina Jackson

Consultant Dermatologist

Dr Katherine Acland
Dr Clive Archer
Dr Natalie Attard
Prof Jonathan Barker
Dr Richard Barlow
Dr Emma Benton
Dr Fiona Child
Dr Emma Craythorne
Dr Nemesha Desai
Dr Hiva Fassihi
Dr David Fenton
Dr Carsten Flohr
Dr Clive Grattan
Dr Richard Groves
Dr Katie Lacy
Dr Fiona Lewis
Dr Raj Mallipeddi
Dr John McFadden
Prof John McGrath
Dr Jemima Mellerio
Prof Frank Nestle
Dr Robert Sarkany
Dr Nisith Sheth
Prof Catherine Smith
Dr Mary Wain

Dr Emma Wedgeworth
Dr Jonathan White
Dr Ian White
Prof Sean Whittaker

Deputy CNS

Ms Mabel Allieu

Dermatopathologist

Dr Eduardo Calonje
Dr Blanca Martin
Dr Alistair Robson
Dr Catherine Stefanato

**Dermatopathology
Laboratory Staff**

Mr Pushpharan Balachandran
Mrs Cansu Bulut
Mrs Patricia Fernando
Mr Jeyrroy Gabriel
Mrs Effrosyni Georgaki
Mrs Fiona Ismail
Mr Theddeus Nwokie
Dr Guy Orchard
Mr Chris-Jude Quaye
Ms Zainab Ramji
Mr Mohamed Shams
Mrs Joanne Torres
Ms Karolina Wojcik

**Dermatopathology
Office Manager**

Mrs Saffron Blake

**Emeritus Professor/Retired
Honorary Staff**

Prof Martin Black
Prof Stanley Bleehen
Prof Robin Eady
Prof Malcolm Greaves
Dr Andrew Griffiths
Prof John Hawk
Dr Anne Kobza Black
Dr Sallie Neill
Dr Richard Rycroft

**Epidermolysis Bullosa
Laboratory Staff**

Ms Sophia Aristodemou
Ms Trish Dopping-Hepenstal
Dr Lu Liu
Dr James McMillan
Ms Humeira Mehter
Ms Linda Ozoemena

GRIDA Management

Mr James Audley
Ms Jo Elias
Mr Olaf Hartberg
Mr Jon Melbourne

**Head of Nursing/
Deputy Head of Nursing**

Ms Maija Hansen
Mr Clarence Moore

Honorary Consultant Staff

Dr Piu Banerjee
Dr Elizabeth Derrick
Dr Sinead Langan
Dr Francis Lawlor
Dr Tabi Leslie
Dr Rajini Mahendran
Dr Andrew Markey
Dr David McGibbon
Dr Helené Menage
Dr Ljubomir Novakovic
Dr Jane Setterfield

Immunodermatology Laboratory Staff

Mr Balbir Bhogal
Mr Pete Carrington
Dr John Mee
Mrs Chinele Ukachukwau
Mrs Joanne Warrick

Matrons

Ms Charlotte Adjei
Ms Ann Bowrin-Soyer
Ms Belma Linic

Mycology Laboratory Staff

Mr Martin Cunningham
Ms Helen Hoey
Dr Susan Howell

Nursing Assistants

Ms Sylvia Koffi
Ms Halyna Kolisnichenko

Ms Angela Lamont
Ms Bashererat Martins
Ms Henryka Szoltysik
Ms Patricia Taylor

Patient Pathway Managers

Ms Anoju Devi
Ms Rachel Driver
Mr Ian Hendry
Mr Jeremy Mashonga
Ms Shantie Scipio
Ms Julie Wright

Photosensitivity Practitioners

Ms Hasha Naik
Ms Susan Walker

Psychologist

Mr Mark Turner
Ms Danuta Orlowska

Psychotherapists

Mrs Katherine Moss

Reception Team Leader

Mrs Sonia Flinch

KCL Non Clinical Academic

Prof Anthony Young

Educational Administrator

Mr Jaime Biggs

MSc Course Administrator

Ms Elena de Teran

Research Staff: KCL Research Assistants

Ms Sara Lombardi
Ms Kylie Morgan
Ms Rashida Pramanik

Research Staff: KCL Laboratory Managers

Mr Michael Allen
Ms Felicia Hunte
Ms Bethan Jones

Research Staff: KCL Research Manager

Mr Robert Pleass

Research Staff: KCL Technicians

Ms Isabel Correa
Ms Katarzyna Grys
Ms Kristina Ilieva
Ms Isabella Tosi

KCL Research Staff: Personal Assistants

Ms Sandra Grant
Mrs Val Hill
Ms Dawn Joseph

Research Staff: BRC Nurse

Ms Magda Martinez
Ms Hemawtee Sreeneebus
Ms Kate Thornberry

Research Staff: KCL Senior Lecturers

Ms Francesca Capon
Ms Sophia Karagainnis

Research Staff: KCL Senior Post-Doctoral

Ms Heather Bax
Mr Anthony Cheung
Mr Michael Simpson

Research Staff: KCL Senior Secretary

Ms Joann Johnson

Research Staff: KCL Administrative Assistant

Mr Damilola Fajuyigbe

Research Staff: KCL Project Manager

Mr Graham Harrison

Research Staff: KCL Database Developer

Ms Tejus Desandi

Secretarial/Administrative Staff

Ms Remi Adesina
Ms Jean Adly
Ms Alison Andrew
Ms Frances Boudjemaa
Ms Nicole Brooks
Ms Brenda Bush
Ms Ana Maria Castro
Ms Sarah Cobb
Ms Janice Cronin
Ms Maria Csaszar
Ms Sophia Cyrille
Ms Samantha de Jonge
Ms Katherine Eccles
Ms Carrie Facer
Ms Penina Goldberg
Mr Afzal Hussain
Mrs Vivienne Jurczynski
Ms Louise Lazarus
Ms Lisa March
Ms Susan Mitchelson
Ms Hana Pearson
Ms Susan Phillips
Ms Elizabeth Pierce
Ms Roshane Robinson
Ms Rebecca Roles
Ms Tessa Ross
Ms Pooja Sampat
Mrs Theresa Samuel
Ms Elorine Shields-Smith
Ms Shelly Smith
Ms Natalie Spring-Brown
Mrs Carol Udo
Ms Alicia Vidal

Ms Linda Watson
Mrs Lorraine Monteiro
Ms Sandra Rama

Senior Nursing assistants

Mr Rahul Ahmed
Ms Erica Barbose de Almeida
Ms Hirut Fekade
Ms Angela Levene
Ms Jane Moore
Ms Richard Thornley

Senior Staff Nurses

Ms Lydia Awosode
Ms Genevieve Concha
Ms Rosana Delgano
Ms Rosalyn Dona
Mrs Maricel Franco
Ms Marissa Garcia-Cruz
Ms Anna Glendinning
Ms Divina Guerrero
Ms Monika Gyimesi
Ms Sunny Hizon
Ms Tita Kebede
Ms Karel Nevill
Ms Anna Palmitessa
Ms Candice Pyke
Ms Jane Smith

Skin Tumour Laboratory Staff

Mr Carl Beyers
Ms Silvia Ferreira
Dr Tracey Mitchell
Ms Vidhya Pararajasingam

Sister

Ms Caroline Immanuel
Ms Erin Mewton
Ms Manda Mootien-Woolterton
Ms Gillian Ogden
Ms Emily-Jo Rodger

Staff Nurses

Ms Maria Akinde
Ms Lisa Beyer
Ms Dzoulia Ibara Ngatse
Mr Gary McCreevy

Affiliated Consultant Staff: Oncologists:

Dr Mark Harries
Dr Stephen Morris

Plastic Surgeon:

Mrs Jenny Geh
Mr Ciaran Healy
Mr Alastair MacKenzie-Ross

Affiliated Emeritus Professor/Retired:

Dr Margaret Spittle

Acknowledgements for illustrations in this book

Every effort has been made to locate the owners of copyrighted material, or their heirs or assigns, to seek permission to reproduce those images whose copyright does not reside with St John's Institute of Dermatology. We are grateful to the individuals and institutions who have assisted in this task. Any omissions are entirely unintentional we would be grateful for any information that would allow us to correct any errors or omissions in a subsequent edition of the work.

Chapter 1

St John's Institute of Dermatology (p8) The Hospital at Leicester Square (2), The Hospital at 5 Lisle Street, St Thomas' Hospital (p9) John Laws Milton (p12) Three Moulages (p13) John Macleod (p14) Honours Board at Lisle Street, Dr Etain Cronin in the Contact Clinic (p15) Geoffrey Dowling, Charles Calnan, Ian Magnus, First edition of Dermatitis (Charles Calnan) (p16) Cartoon by Dr Neil Smith, 1992 (p17) HRH The Princess Royal opening the Institute of Dermatology, Dermatology Institute Sign (p18) Scientific research, DNA sequence, Research laboratory.

Guy's and St Thomas' Hospital (p17) Postgraduate training.

King's College London (p8) The Hospital at Guy's.

iStock PhotoLibrary (p18) Stem Cell 25815091.

Public Domain and Creative Commons Licensed Images (p7) Dermatitis histiology (ref. Dermnet Skin Disease Atlas) (p10) William Tilbury Fox (ref. Rovi Data Solutions), Erasmus Wilson, Leicester Square in 1874 (p11) Cartoon published in Judy, 1899, Herpes Gestations (ref. Wikimedia Commons), Urticaria Pigmentosa (ref. skinpathology.org), (p12) Robert Koch (ref. Wikipedia.org) (p13) Sir Malcolm Morris (ref. V&A Laffayette), Dr. James Herbert Stowers (ref. British Association of Dermatologists), Sir Ernest Graham Little (ref. National Portrait Gallery), Lupus Vulgaris patient (ref. Wikimedia Commons), Lupus Vulgaris histiology (ref. Indian Dermatology Online) (p15) Malcolm Greaves (ref. London Allergy Clinic), Urticaria pigmentosa (skinpathology.org), Irritant contact dermatitis (ref. dermpedia.org), Protoporphyria (ref. Geneva Foundation for Medical Education and Research) (p19) BRAF and RAS - mutation in the nucleus (ref. Marius Geanta, BRF0000531200).

Illustrations by AYA-Creative (p19) BRAF and RAS - mutation in the nucleus (ref. Marius Geanta, BRF0000531200).

Chapter 2

St John's Institute of Dermatology (p23) Geoffrey Dowling, Bob Meara, George Wells, Robin Eady (p26) Family pedigree, Affected individual II-2 with skin crusting, Exph 5 patient (Richardson's stain), Mutation in Exophilin 5 low-magnification transmission electron micrograph (ref. National Center for Biotechnology Information) (p27) Immunofluorescence in Epidermolysis bullosa acquisita skin, Sophie the Countess of Wessex with EB patient (p32) Bethan Thomas (p33) Mandy Aldwin.

Guy's and St Thomas' Hospital (p24) Testing Samples (p28) Analysing skin biopsies (p32) Preparing dressing.

iStock PhotoLibrary, Shutterstock Library, Stock Photolibrary (p21) Genetic Modification 17536862 (p22) Chromosome Mutation 1792275 (p25) Reading genetic code.

Public Domain and Creative Commons Licensed Images (p22) Ichthyosis (ref. dermquest.com), Ichthyosis Vulgaris (ref. dermquest.com), Lichen Sclerosis (ref. Online Dermatology Clinic), Ichthyosis Vulgaris histiology (ref. DermPedia.org), Lichen Sclerosus (ref. WikiMedia.org) Extracellular matrix matrix protein 1 (ref. John McGrath: National Library of Medicine) (p23) John McGrath (ref. ttaregistration.co.uk), Collagen VII in normal skin and EB skin (ref. wenxinwang.ie) (p24) Polymerase chain reaction (ref. Wikipedia), Immunohistochemistry and immunofluorescence (ref. Leinco Technologies) (p25) Desmosome, Epithelia-Cell junction (ref. Antranik.org), Plakophilin 1 Protein (ref. Wikipedia) (p26) Family pedigree, Affected individual II-2 with skin crusting, Exph 5 patient (Richardson's stain), Mutation in Exophilin 5 low-magnification transmission electron micrograph (ref. National Centre for Biotechnology Information) (p27) Immunofluorescense in EB (ref. Medscape) (p29) Human fibroblast cells injected into EB patient (Stephanie Saade) (p30) The molecular basis of inherited skin blistering involving hemidesmosome-associated proteins (ref. National Centre for Biotechnology Information), Revertant mosaicism in RDEB (ref. National Center for Biotechnology Information) (p31) The autologous transplant process (ref. Lymphomation.org), Induced pluripotent stem cell therapy (ref. EuroStemCell.org).

Illustrations by AYA-Creative (p22) Extracellular matrix matrix protein 1 (ref. John McGrath: National Library of Medicine) (p23) Collagen VII in normal skin and EB skin (ref. wenxinwang.ie) (p24) Polymerase chain reaction (ref. Wikipedia), Immunohistochemistry and immunofluorescence (ref. Leinco Technologies) (p25) Desmosome, Epithelia-Cell junction (ref. Antranik.org) (p26) Family pedigree (p30) The molecular basis of inherited skin blistering involving hemidesmosome-associated proteins (ref. National Centre for Biotechnology Information) (p31) The autologous transplant process (ref. Lymphomation.org), Induced pluripotent stem cell therapy (ref. EuroStemCell.org).

Chapter 3

St John's Institute of Dermatology (p37) Patient with chronic actinic dermatitis (p38) Mrs Harsha Naik phototesting using the monochromator, Positive phototests in a patient with chronic actinic dermatitis (p39) UVA1 phototherapy machine, UVA1 phototherapy machine and team (p40) Patient with vitiligo before and after treatment (p41) Nodular cirrhotic liver, Porphyria cutanea tarda, Nodular cirrhotic liver (p42) Dr Mieran Sethi – MRC-funded XP Research Fellow 2014-2017 (p43) Dr Hiva Fassihi, Clinical Lead of the UK National XP Service with an XP patient, (p46) UVA1 and UVB fluorescence microscopy showing damage to DNA, UVA and UVB rays (p47) Nucleotide excision repair pathway.

Guy's and St Thomas' Hospital (p45) Eddison Miller in UVR Protective Clothing, Eddison Miller's "indoor garden"(p46) Eddison Miller.

iStock PhotoLibrary (p35) The Sun 5145958 (p36) Couple sunbathing on the beach 24199011.

Public Domain and Creative Commons Licensed Images (p36) UVA and UVB rays (ref. Spot on Solutions) Testing skin under normal and ultra violet light (ref. cnet.com) (p37) Niels Finsen (ref. The Nobel Foundation 1903), Finsen lamp treatment 1925 (ref. Wikimedia Commons), UV Light Spectrum (ref. Aquanetto) (p38) Ultraviolet radiation separated into individual wavelength (ref. Physics Stack Exchange) (p40) Left arm of a scleroderma patient (ref. Wikipedia) (p41) Porphyria cutanea tarda: skin histiology (ref. dermaamin.com).

Illustrations by AYA-Creative (p36) UVA and UVB rays (ref. Spot on Solutions) (p37) UV Light Spectrum (ref. Aquanetto) (p38) Ultraviolet radiation separated into individual wavelength (ref. Physics Stack Exchange) (p46) UVA and UVB rays penetrating skin (ref. etquefaire.fr) (p47) Nucleotide excision repair pathway (ref. St John's Institute of Dermatology).

Chapter 4

St John's Institute of Dermatology (p50) Kathleen Morrey before surgery, Kathleen Morrey after surgery, Kathleen Morrey with Dr Raj Mallipeddi, Kathleen today (p51) Emma Craythorne (p52) Christopher Zachary (p52) Confocal scanning microscopes in use, Nisith Sheth (p56) Ann Layton, Richard Barlow with Pulsed Dye Laser (p57) The Q-switched laser (p58) In-vivo reflectance confocal microscope (p59) Emma Craythorne using the in-vivo reflectance confocal microscope.

iStock Photolibrary (p49) Blue laser 2748002.

Public Domain and Creative Commons Licensed Images (p52) Frederic Mohs (ref. Paul W. Marino) (p53) Seeing into the skin at different depths (ref. Spie Digital Library), Lentigno maligna histiology (ref. Dermpedia.org), Dermatofibrosarcoma orotuberans histiology (ref. Christopher Beauchamp: Orthopaedics One) (p57) Pulsed Dye Laser (ref. Syneron Candela) (p58) Fractional scanner pattern of C02 Laser (ref. NewSurg.com) (p59) In-vivo reflectance confocal microscopic images (ref. Spie Digital Library).

Illustrations by AYA-Creative (p54-55) Mohs surgery: the process (ref. Seacoast Skin Surgery) (p57) Pulsed Dye Laser (ref. Syneron Candela).

Chapter 5

St John's Institute of Dermatology (p62) Melanoma, Influence of combinations of three different mutations, Cases of melanoma and deaths per annum (p64) Group Photo of the team (p65) Sentinel nodes map (ref. Terese Winslow, U.S. Gov, uchospitals.edu), Lymph node biopsy, Surgeon operating lymph node (p67) BRAF and its effect on cell cycle (p68) Mole Mapping, Skin cancer tissue bank (p69) Hedgehog Signalling Pathway, Margaret Spittle (p70) Abnormal chromosomes from a patient with a cutaneous lymphoma, Cutaneous lymphoma cell in blood, Electron microscopy image of abnormal nucleus, Lymphoma cells in skin (p71) Tomotherapy for mycosis fungoides (2), Total Skin Election Beam Therapy (3) (p72-3) Stem cell transplants, Clinical treatment effect of extracorporeal photochemotherapy inpatients, Extracorporeal photopheresis (p74) Martin Gammon and wife (p75) Genetic Mapping.

King's College London (p75) Human genome sequencing.

iStock Photolibrary (p61) Melanoma under microscope 019794886 (p62) Sun exposure 59462992 (p75) Genetic screening 14969967.

Public Domain and Creative Commons Licensed Images (p63) Melanoma driven by BRAF and NRAS gene mutations (ref. Krishan Maggon), PET scans of patients treated with vermurofenib (ref. G. McArthur and R. Hicks, Peter MacCallum Cancer Centre) (p64) Melanoma progression (ref. Jenna Rebelo, pathophys.org) (p66) Spect CT (ref. Prof. M. Hacker), Spect CT scanning (ref. jnm.snmjournals.org) (p72-3) Stem cell transplant (ref. Eric Vivier, Sophie Ugolini, Didier Blaise, Christian Chabannon & Laurent Brossay) (p75) Metastatic Melanoma cell (ref. National Cancer Institute Nci-vol-9872-300).

Illustrations by AYA-Creative (p62) Influence of combinations of three different mutations (ref. St. John's Institute) (p63) Melanoma driven by BRAF and NRAS gene mutations (ref. Krishan Maggon) (p64) Melanoma progression (ref. Jenna Rebelo, pathophys.org) (p65) Sentinel nodes map (ref. Terese Winslow, U.S. Gov, uchospitals.edu) (p67) BRAF and its effect on cell cycle (ref. St. John's Institute of Dermatology) (p69) Hedgehog Signalling Pathway (ref. St. John's Institute) (p71) Total Skin Election Beam Therapy (ref. St. John's Institute of Dermatology) (p72-3) Stem cell transplant (ref. Eric Vivier, Sophie Ugolini, Didier Blaise, Christian Chabannon & Laurent Brossay), Extracorporeal photopheresis (ref. St. John's Institute of Dermatology) (p75) Genetic Mapping (ref. St. John's Institute of Dermatology).

Chapter 6

St John's Institute of Dermatology (p79) The Psoriasis Team, Clinical care (p83) Bullous pemphigoid (p85) Malcolm Greaves (p87) Marjorie Ridley (p89) John West.

iStock Photolibrary (p77) White Blood Cells 14513135 (p78) Inflammatory skin disease 14513135 (p79) Blood testing 23876398, 27484845 (p80) Blood testing 55770966 (p84) Chronic urticaria 17918464 (p85) Chronic spontaneous urticaria 40839398 (p87) Cream application 154751.

Public Domain and Creative Commons Licensed Images (p78) Normal and psoriasis skin (ref. Galderma.com) (p80) Psoriasis plaque before and after treatment (ref. crutchfielddermatology.com) (p81) 4 stages of psoriasis (ref. J Clin Invest: The American Society for Clinical Investigation) (p82) Bullous pemphigoid (ref. hellomrdoctor.com), Pemphigus vulgaris (ref. DrSamuel L Moschella MD FACP: dermpedia.org) (p85) Histamine release and degranulation (ref. mol-biol4masters.masters.grkraj.org), Chronic spontaneous urticaria (ref. Artur Zembowicz M.D. Ph.D.: dermpedia.org), Clive Grattan (ref. guysandstthomasevents.co.uk) (p86) Omalizumab - biologic drug for chronic urticaria (ref. Stephen T. Holgate & Riccardo Polosa: nature.com) (p87) Lichen sclerosus (ref. wikimedia.org) (p88) Hidradenitis suppurativa - histology (ref. aocd-grandrounds.org), illustration (ref. Stewart EG: macklin.org.uk) and patient (2) (ref. dermaamin.com).

Illustrations by AYA-Creative (p78) Normal and psoriasis skin (ref. Galderma.com) (p81) 4 stages of psoriasis (ref. J Clin Invest: The American Society for Clinical Investigation) (p85) Histamine release and degranulation (p85) Histamine release and degranulation (ref. mol-biol4masters.masters.grkraj.org) (p86) Omalizumab - biologic drug for chronic urticaria (ref. Stephen T. Holgate & Riccardo Polosa: nature.com) (p88) Hidradenitis suppurativa illustration (ref. Stewart EG: macklin.org.uk).

Chapter 7

St John's Institute of Dermatology (p94) Patch testing - the Finn Chamber technique (p95) Anna Glendinning with patient (p96) Etain Cronin, Patch Tests printed results (p97) Richard Rycroft (p98) Ian White, John McFadden, Jonathan White, Piu Banerjee, (p99) Range of cosmetics (p100) Tree moss (Evernia furfuracea), Oak moss (Evernia prunastri) (p101) Baseline series, Contact Dermatitis Journals (p104) Allergic contact dermatitis, Patient with a contact allergy.

L.A. Stone, E.M. Lindfield, S.Robertson (p94) Wheal – urticaria (p97) Contact dermatitis - clothing, Atopic eczema, Jewellery allergy

iStock Photolibrary (p91) Crushed eyeshadow powder 36638730 (p92) Woman with acne 37341210 (p93) Asthma 34912030, Hay fever 53303389, Dust mites 39737356, Urticaria 40839398 (p98) Brick laying 25928423 (p92,99,102,105) Methylisothiazolinone in cosmetics, perfumes and hair dyes, hand washing, cosmetics and household products 1405273, 16699368, 20953939, 6101493, 26636974, 12514154, 19267618, 45154888, 38816124, 41823884, 13409913, 16794539 (p100) Tangerine Oil 27035876 (p101) Nurse in mask 19557464 (p102) Nickel allergy 22716609 (p103) Hair dyeing 9088288, Dyed hair colours 50876194, Severe dermatitis 11769756.

Public Domain and Creative Commons Licensed Images (p92) Methylisothiazolinone (ref. commons.wikimedia.org) (p93) 4 types of allergic reaction (ref. Fauquier ENT: fauquierent.blogspot.co.uk) (p94) Irritant contact dermatitis histology (ref. Dermatology Online Journal: escholarship.org), Eczema - histology (ref. Dermnet.com and the Dermnet Skin Disease Atlas) Hyperkeratosis histology (ref. Wikipedia.org) (p96) Alitretynoin (ref. wikipedia.org) (p97) Alitretinoin (ref.

commons.wikimedia.org), Mechanism of action of ciclosporin (ref. Expert Reviews in Molecular Medicine: Cambridge University Press) (p100) Atranol (ref. chemsynthesis.com), Hydroxyisohexyl (ref. Wikipedia.org), Lemon myrtle (ref. en.wikipedia.org) (p101) Methylisothiazolinone (ref. commons.wikimedia.org) (p102) Nickel allergy located on the ear (ref. Jene Mammino, DO: aocd.org), Nickel allergy on the neck (ref. aniaostudio-istockphoto), 5p nickel coins (ref. Anna Lacey BBCHealth Check: bbc.co.uk) (p103) Toxic sofa (ref. thesun.co.uk).

AYA Creative (p92) Methylisothiazolinone (ref. commons.wikimedia.org) (p93) Skin prick test - application and reaction reaction (2), 4 types of allergic reaction (ref. Fauquier ENT: fauquierent.blogspot.co.uk) (p96) Allergens stored, Allergens prepared in syringes, Finn Chambers being filled, Filled Finn Chambers (p97) Mechanism of action of ciclosporin (ref. Expert Reviews in Molecular Medicine: Cambridge University Press) (p99) Nurse washing hands (p100) Atranol (ref. chemsynthesis.com), Hydroxyisohexyl (ref. Wikipedia.org) (p101) Methylisothiazolinone (ref. commons.wikimedia.org) (p103) Dimethyl fumarate (ref. commons.wikimedia.org).

Chapter 8

St John's Institute of Dermatology (p110) Karina Jackson, Surgeon with patient (p111) Nurse with laser, Phototherapy treatment, Light box, Children with EB (p112) Skin cancer screening (p113) Iontophoresis treatment for hyperhidrosis (p114) Maija Hansen, Nurse with mother and child (p115) Nurse delivering ECP, The ECP suite (p118) Nurse with ultrasound, St. John's nurse undertaking specialist training course.

Guy's and St Thomas' Hospital (p108) Edward Ward at St Thomas' in the 1950s, Dermatology nurses with patient (p109) Nurse with patient (p110) Dermatology Day Centre treatment pictures (5) (p112) Photodynamic therapy (p120, p121, p122) The Bermondsey Centre at Guy's.

King's College London (p117) Alopecia patient Jaiden.

L.A. Stone, E.M. Lindfield, S.Robertson (p111) Clinical care (p112) Atopic eczema, Nodular prurigo, EB patient (p116) Use of emollients (2) (p118) Lynette Stone, A Colour Atlas of Nursing Procedures in Skin Disorders.

iStock Photolibrary, Shutterstock Photolibrary (p107) Ampoules 21356990 (p109) Administration of injection 161947730 (p116) Small chemical glass bottles 25555567 (117) Skin disease patient 21547591.

Public Domain and Creative Commons Licensed Images (p111) Melanoma (ref. Wikipedia.org) (p112) Nurses support families of children5with EB (ref. Debra.org) (p112) Extra corporeal photopheresis (ref. NHS Rotherham Photopheresis Unit) (p116) Hamamelis - Witch Hazel (ref. Garden Oasis.co.uk)

Illustrations AYA-Creative (p111) Diagnostic tests for allergy (p115) Extra corporeal photopheresis (ref. NHS Rotherham Photopheresis Unit) (p116) Mercury.